Grill Cookbook for Beginners

Learn the Fundamentals of Grilling and 85+ Delicious Recipes to Enjoy Your Summer Grilling Season

LARS J.

Table of Content

Introduction

Grilling food on an open fire is one of life's greatest pleasures if done properly. A grill is a piece of cooking equipment that consists of an open grate or rack that serves as the cooking surface and a heating element underneath. Depending on the grill type, the heat source can be open flame (charcoal or gas) or electric. Grills come in various shapes and sizes, ranging from a simple 20 dollars charcoal grill to a 15,000 dollars gas grill, but the basics remain consistent. In the 2000s, grilling technology progressed. As the patent on infrared grills expires, they become less expensive, but they remain prohibitively expensive for most consumers and are not widely accessible. In 2004, Big, a Discovery Channel show, built the world's largest grill. It is capable of grilling a ten-foot-long hotdog from a height of more than fifteen feet! In the last decade, small portable gas grills have become common for picnicking. Over the years, there have been many advancements in the way people prepare food, most notably how they grill their meat. Grills have evolved from unreliable and messy cooking methods to a soothing and common way of cooking globally. Because food is cooked directly on the grill's grate or rack, the best foods to grill are meats and poultry, while firm fish, seafood, and vegetables can also be grilled. Due to the fact that a grill cooks with dry heat at a high temperature, grilled meats can have juicy cuts, and marinating helps retain moisture in the meat.

When summer approaches, the majority of people can fire up the grill in their backyard. Grilling is renowned for its robust, smoky taste and perfectly charred surfaces formed by a hot grill grate, and it is ideal for cooking thin, quick-cooking foods. A grill pan may be used to achieve this effect. Although a grill pan's elevated ridges may result in grill marks, purists argue that cooking at a grill pan is not grilling. The distinctive flavor of grilled food comes from the drippings, not the fuel. As the oils, carbohydrates, and proteins in the drippings came into contact with the heat source below, they exploded into flames and smoke. The heat creates new complex molecules that emerge in the smoke and the warm air surrounding the food you're grilling. Since the invention of cooking, there have been numerous methods for preparing and serving meals. All of these approaches can result in a variety of distinct taste sensations, adding to the enjoyment of dinnertime. Grilling, especially for barbecue, is a common method of cooking. This is how the popularity of this form of cooking developed. When it comes to cooking, it is primarily about the temperature. To get the best results, most professional grillers understand how to control their grill's temperature. This book will teach you all the fundamentals you need to know before embarking on your journey and will also provide you with some delectable recipes to try along the way. Give this book a try; you will undoubtedly discover a great deal more about grilling and its benefits.

Chapter 1: Grilling And Its Basics

Grilling is something we've all grown up seeing our parents do before we can remember. We used to be mesmerized by watching those fat hot dogs plump up and burst open while we were young (if you had natural casing dogs). Remember the aroma of beef from those thick, juicy burgers, all that fat pouring onto the gleaming red coals with a hiss, a blast of flames, and blue smoke twirling around the blazing hot edges? It is now fun to see your children's or grandchildren's faces light up as they watch you turn burgers with some style and showmanship. Grilling may be considered an instinct. It is in our blood almost from the moment we're born.

1.1 What is Grilling?

According to the scientific version, grilling is a fast, dry heat cooking process that uses a "large amount of direct, radiant heat," according to the scientific understanding. Direct conduction heating is used while cooking in a pan or skillet, while grilling is thermal radiation. Grilling temperatures often reach 260°C/500°F, making this a fast-cooking process that must be closely monitored. Otherwise, the freshly fried hot dogs can quickly transform into road flares. The browning of sugars and proteins on meat and vegetables, which produces the beautiful coloration and additional flavor profile, is what really makes grilled foods taste better. The Maillard reaction occurs as foods exceed temperatures over 155 °C/310 °F, and it causes browning. Grilling is a simple three-step process – A barbecue, some beef, and fire are required, but no special equipment. Of course, there's a lot more to study, including several grilling tips and tricks that will help you improve your game, but those three things are the most important. Nothing improves the taste of meat quite like fire and smoke. That's what there is to it. Bring back memories of your childhood and turn up the barbecue!

The Mycenaean culture of ancient Greece, about 1600 B.C., was the first to demonstrate that man knows how to throw a tailgate party. Rectangular ceramic trays were found during archaeological excavations. Julie Hruby, a Dartmouth College assistant professor of classics, experimented with reconstructing such ancient clay trays to understand their use better. They turned out to be heavy but lightweight ceramic grills with a tray that contained coals for cooking skewered beef. In Greece, it is known as souvlaki, and in other parts of the world, it is known as Shish-Kabob. Weight wasn't a problem back then since they had servants and oxen. Fortunately, now there are pickup trucks, SUVs, and lightweight metal grills that you can carry with you wherever you go. Actual grilling consists of cooking food on an opened wire grid with the fire either above or below the food. Broiling is the term we use where the heat source is above, but it also falls within the concept of grilling.

1.2 Difference between grilling and BBQ

Can you understand the difference between grilling and barbecuing? Both methods produce delicious food, but there is a significant difference between them. Summer has arrived, and everybody is venturing out of their kitchens and into their decks to cook. Is it grilling, or is it barbecuing? Does it make a difference? Is there a distinction? And though we use the terms "barbecue" and "grill" interchangeably, there is a distinction to be made between the two. It really does matter if you are a genuine outdoor chef!

The cooking time and temperature are the significant differences in grilling and barbecuing. Grilling involves fast cooking over high heat, while barbecuing involves slow cooking over a long period using low, indirect heat. Each cooking process needs different equipment (though you can, confusingly, smoke on the grills and grill on some smokers.) The consistency of the meat is another crucial distinction between the two cooking processes. Tough and fatty meats need a lengthy, slow cooking phase to break down the collagen and other tissues, resulting in moist, tender beef. That's why you can barbecue with larger and inexpensive cuts. Lean or tender beef, chicken, and seafood, on the other hand, need rapid cooking over high heat to reach a safe internal temperature without drying out.

Grilling:

This is what most families do for dinner in their backyards. This is also what most people mean when they say "barbecue." Grilling is the process of preparing foods quickly and in a hot environment (usually 500-550 degrees Fahrenheit, or even higher). It is usually done over extreme heat. Grill able meats include steaks, seafood, pork chops, hamburgers, and hot dogs. Many vegetables and fruits are also delicious when grilled. Grilling takes place over the intense fire, with the flame (gas or charcoal) immediately under the meat.

Barbecuing:

Barbecuing is the process of frying food at a low temperature over an extended period. Barbecuing is often used for meat cuts such as ribs, beef brisket, pork shoulder, and whole chickens or turkeys. These meats are harder and need the medium, slow heat of a barbecue (or a slow cooker) to become tender. Barbecued food is cooked for an extended period at a shallow temperature (usually 225 ° F or lower) (hours, or even all day long).

Barbecuing is often performed using indirect fire, in which the heat supply is connected to the chamber in which the meat is held, so the meat is not entirely over the flames, as is the case with a grill. The heat source for a barbecue is usually charcoal or wood. Multiple forms of wood emit various smoky flavors, which the meat may absorb. The best barbecue chefs take pleasure in using a long cooking period to get the most tender, tasty meat.

Here's a fast reference if you are still undecided on which meat to use:

Grilling	Barbecue
Hot dogs and sausages	Whole hams and pork shoulders
Fish, oysters, and shrimp on the half shell	Ribs of pork or beef
Hamburgers	Beef brisket
Chops and steaks	Whole or half goat, pig, or beef
Boneless chicken, duck, or turkey	Whole chickens, turkey and duck

1.3 Types of Grills

We all know that there is a range of heating and fuel choices available while grilling. These fuel sources have their combination of benefits and drawbacks, with several having the ability to affect the overall taste of the food you prepared. Let's take a deeper look at some of the numerous grills that use both of these fuel supplies. There are various ways to classify the world's dozens, and perhaps hundreds, of different grills. You may categorize them based on the type of fuel they use, such as charcoal grills, gas grills and wood burning grills. You may group them by areas of origin, such as South American grills or Southeast Asian grills. However, from a griller's perspective, the most helpful method is to arrange the fire and place the food for cooking. This is what decides the temperature at which the food can grill and how easily it can cook. Understanding and monitoring these factors can determine how effective you are as a grill master. The major types of grills are:

1. Charcoal Grills

For a variety of reasons, charcoal grills have long been a favorite of outdoor cooks. A charcoal grill is simple to use, and foodies adore the smoky, rich taste that charcoal provides. There are a few things that all charcoal grills have in common. The air intake is situated at the bottom of the grill and can be manually adjusted. When air enters the grill, it travels through the lit charcoal and escapes through a second vent at the top, identical to a wood-burning stove. The hotter the grill becomes; the more air can penetrate and leave it. One of the advantages of controlling the air intake and exhaust is that if the temperature stabilizes inside the temperature zone you choose to cook at. It usually stays there during the cooking period, as long as there is enough charcoal to sustain it going at that temperature. This is especially useful when cooking tougher cuts of meat over long periods because it helps them break down into tender meat with intense flavors.

2. Charcoal kettle grills

One of the more well-known types of charcoal grills is the kettle grill. They're plain, shaped like a kettle, consisting of a rounded bottom, a tight stand, removable lid, and grill grates. Charcoal is put in the grill's bottom compartment, raised on a small grate to allow ash and other cooking debris to spill quickly away from the heat source while ensuring an even airflow over the coals. One of the key advantages of this style of the grill is its portability. Kettle grills are typically constructed of metal and are low in weight. They come in a variety of sizes, but they're primarily portable and require less charcoal.

3. Kamado grills

Kamado grills, also known as the ceramic smokers or the egg grills, are a more modern variant of the traditional charcoal grill that has become increasingly common in recent years. Kamado grills operate on similar concepts to kettle grills but with a few key exceptions. The design of the kamado grill is more elongated, like the form of an eggshell. They are much stronger than a kettle grill since they are constructed of a more rigid ceramic substance and can weigh anywhere from 150 to 500 pounds based on the size.

Like the kettle grill, air movement and temperature are regulated via the bottom and top of the grill, but because of its thermal mass and more engineered design, even minor adjustments on a kamado grill will significantly temperature changes. The lid or dome is not usually removed entirely due to the kamado grill's width and weight and is attached to the grill's base with heavy-duty, spring-loaded hinges.

The kamado grill can normally pre-heat for about 45 minutes to an hour until the charcoal is lit to get its thick walls up to the temperature you want before cooking. It generates less ash than manufactured charcoal briquettes by using all natural hardwood lump charcoal as a source of heat. Hardwood lump charcoal, according to some grilling and barbecuing lovers, has the best flavor. While kamado grills excel as a source of scorching food, their flexibility in cooking appeals to many people; the heat deflector is a popular kamado grill accessory. It resembles a hard pizza stone which acts as a barrier between the food and the hot charcoal. The use of a heat deflector enables this type of grill to cook more like an oven, transferring heat from all directions to your food. This results in a steadier heat and more minor hot spots, which is ideal for baking anything from cheesecakes to pizzas; imagination is the only limit.

4. Pellet grills

While pellet grills have been around for about 30 years, they have become a popular grilling choice in the last five years due to their convenience and flavor. One of the most enticing aspects of the pellet grill is that it can be used both as a grill or smoker, which is a fantastic selling point.

A hopper holds food-grade wood pellets about the diameter of a black-eyed pea, which are auger-delivered to a burn jar. Depending on the temperature you set for your grill, the burn pot and thermostat operate together electronically to maintain the temperature. There aren't many changes to make after you have the grill running to your standards. The electronic temperature sensors are continuously changing to keep the grill within the defined range.

This is particularly useful for longer cooks like ribs, brisket, and large roasts since it allows you to leave the meat on its own to cook. This grill style does need a power source, which must be linked during the whole cook and cool-down period due to the electronic settings.

This grill has had a reputation for not browning or searing meat as much as other grills, but certain manufacturers are working hard to shift the image. They are displaying recipes with excellent char and grill marks to change the perception.

5. Gas and Propane grills

According to the Hearth Patio and Barbecue Association (HPBA), 72 percent of American households have a grill, and more than 200 million people can cook outside. Most of these grills are using natural gas or propane, and there are various styles to pick from.

Gas and propane grills are similar in use, with burners producing about 40,000 BTUs of heat and three, four, or more burners firing to cook the food from below with indirect or direct heat. Gas grills are desirable because they are compact, heat up quickly, and provide a range of accessory choices to improve the cooking experience. Side burners, lights, dedicated meat searing areas, and integrated food thermometers are examples of devices that mix gimmicks and gadgets, and the market are constantly incorporating innovations. Gas grills, including gas stoves, turn on automatically and take the least amount of time to heat up so you can start grilling. However, this is handy compared to pellet or charcoal grills; gas burns instead cleanly and adds little taste too. Gas grills are the most popular kind of grill in use today in the United States. It is easy to see why; they're functional, efficient, and versatile. Because of how easy they are to use, they are suitable for the casual griller or beginner. A gas grill will easily hit high temperatures and provide gourmet-quality food for the family and friends with little effort.

Gas grills are often very convenient and easy to clean as well. This is a significant plus for the users because the last thing you want to do after a great meal has to scrub a lot of dishes. There are a few common differences within the gas grill variations:

Propane:

Propane or natural gas are used to operate gas grills. Since propane is contained in small tanks and can usually be purchased at the nearby grocery, propane grills are by nature the more portable of the two. Propane grills are simple to use, but you may need to refill the propane tank on time.

Natural gas:

Natural gas grills are commonly used with built-in grills that link to your home's built-in natural gas line. A natural gas link can, however, be used to power several freestanding grills. Natural gas grills remove the need to purchase petrol from the supermarket. You just take it from your home's existing gas pipes.

Infrared grills:

Infrared grills use infrared technology to distribute heat through the entire grilling surface and are fueled by either propane or natural gas. This occurs very quickly, and infrared technology prevents the fire from entering the grates. Infrared grills are known for having zero flare-ups and super-even temperatures, making them ideal for searing as well as "normal" grilling.

Flat top grills:

Flat top grills are characterized by a flat, griddle-like surface and are usually fueled by propane. Flat top grills provide juicier food because no drippings fall below the grates and vaporize. On the other side, flat top grills appear to yield somewhat fewer flavorful results than grills with grates, for the same reason that drippings don't vaporize and smoke back up onto your cooking. Flat top grills are excellent for cooking breakfast, burgers, sautéing vegetables, and several other items.

Freestanding:

The mobility of a freestanding gas grill is a bonus. Since they aren't bound to something or fitted into a cabinet, you can switch them around if needed. Propane or natural gas can be used to fuel freestanding gas grills.

Built-In:

As the name implies, built-in gas grills are built into a permanent structure such as an island cooking platform or cabinet. Built-ins are ideal for anyone wanting to upgrade their outdoor cooking space, and they're usually high-end grills or BBQ islands. You can optimize space efficiency and fit a robust grill into a significant portion of the outdoor kitchen with proper design. Natural gas connections are commonly used to power built-in gas grills.

6. Open grill:

The most common of all grills is a stone or metal box with a wood, charcoal, or propane fire at the bottom and food directly over the fire. The grill grate is not usually required.

It includes table grills from Europe and North America, South American parrillas, the Balkan mangal, the Italian fogolar, the Indonesian sate grill, Asian bucket grills, and the Australian flattop grill, among other stuff. It is used for direct grilling at elevated temperatures. Tiny, tender, quick-cooking foods like kebabs, sates, fish fillets, steaks, chops, vegetables, and so on are best suited.

7. Covered grill:

A covered grill is created by combining an open grill with a tall lid that can be lifted and lowered. While it can seem to be a minor improvement, the closed grill enables you to use two more important live-fire cooking techniques: indirect grilling and smoking. This grill style includes a gas grill, a kettle grill, and a 55-gallon steel-drum grill. It is used for direct grilling of thicker and larger meats and indirect grilling and smoking (the latter done primarily on the charcoal burning grills). The perfect foods for this type of grill are thick steaks, both tuna and beef, veal chops, and double-thick pork. High-fat meats, such as baby back ribs and pork shoulder, and whole chicken and duck, are still the right option.

8. Rotisserie grill:

The rotisserie adds motion to the otherwise static grilling process. A turnspit is slow, gentle rotation evens the cooking process by basting the meat, melting away excess fat, and browning the exterior. Spit-roasted foods are crunchy on the outside and tender on the inside. It Consists of Tuscany and Germany's wood-burning rotisseries, France's gas-wall rotisseries, Malaysia and Singapore's charcoal burning chicken rotisseries, not to mention these infrared rotisseries built into the majority of high-end American gas grills. Vertical rotisseries are used by grill masters in the Middle East and eastern Mediterranean (and elsewhere) to prepare Turkish doner, Greek gyro, and Middle Eastern shawarma. It is used for combining the benefits of both direct and indirect grilling. As with direct grilling, the food is exposed to the heat, but unlike direct grilling, indirect grilling cooks the food next to, rather than directly over, the fire. Cylindrical and fatty foods, such as chicken wings, whole chickens, ducks, rib roasts, and whole hogs, are best suited.

9. Smoker grill:

While smoking is one of the oldest ways of preparing and preserving foods globally, the smoker as a versatile backyard barbecue grill is a twentieth-century North American invention. Every country grills, but not every grill culture smokes. It includes Texas offset barrel smokers, upright water smokers, and box smokers from North America, Europe, China, and pellet/sawdust smokers from North America (such as the Bradley and Traeger). It is used for smoking, indirect grilling with the wood smoke at low to moderate temperatures. The Best-Suited Foods include the following: Historically, it was reserved for tough, tasty meat cuts such as brisket and ribs. (The low, gentle heat softens the collagen, allowing these finicky cuts to be cut with the side of a fork.) To crisp the skin on smoked poultry, you can use "smoke roasting" indirect grilling at the higher temperature.

10. Open pit and Campfire-Style Grills

Originally, grilling (make that cooking) was done over or next to a campfire. This primal method remains extremely popular—particularly in the Americas. It includes the following: Brazil's Fogo de and Argentina's asado, who are both examples of open-pit grilling—meats roasted on stakes in front of a fire. Campfire grilling techniques include the Pacific Northwest's salmon "bakes," Connecticut's planked shad, and roasting marshmallows on sticks to create an American scout favorite: s'mores. It is used for roasting with radiant heat. Whole lamb, pig, goat, salmon, skin-on fish fillets, and rack of beef ribs are all well-suited foods.

1.4 Some grilling styles

Consider your cooking style and space before deciding on the type of grill that is best for your lifestyle.

- **Is your patio or deck electrically connected or within reach of an extension cord?** Without access to a plug-in outlet, a pellet grill is not the best option.

- **Are you providing food for your small army?** Consider some gas options with sufficient cooking space and side burners to keep everything from baked beans to chowder or chili warm and ready to serve whenever the gang is hungry.

- **Do you have adequate space and support for a huge grill?** A kamado grill is a significant weight and space commitment, depending on the size. However, this is an excellent grill to choose.

- **Do you grill on the fly?** If you prefer spontaneity, a slow-heating and stabilizing grill is probably not for you.

- **Are you a purist who would never serve a burger without grill marks and a hint of smokiness?** While gas does not have the best flavor, it is clean, affordable, and quick to heat up.

1.5 Benefits of Grilling

There are health advantages of grilling the meals rather than frying it on the burner or in the oven. Regardless of the temperature, we should all accept that it is always excellent grilling season. From burgers to brats, there are numerous delicious options to sear and savor. The best part is that grilling is not only enjoyable; it can also be beneficial to your health. This topic provides some tips and benefits about how to prepare some delicious and nutritious meals. The best benefits of grilling are as follows:

1. You eat less fat:

You consume less fat while grilling because the fat drips off the grates. Consider grilling a burger rather than frying it in a skillet on the stovetop. The fat renders off on the grill. Since the fat has nowhere to go in a pan on the stovetop, it collects and is finally reabsorbed by the meat.

2. Vegetables on the grill are best suited for you:

The majority of people are unaware that grilling vegetables increase their vitamin and mineral content. This is particularly true for vegetables with low water content. Additionally, vegetables tossed on the grill are typically fresh and seasoned, which is a step up from canned vegetables. Grilled vegetables that are organic and in season are better than canned and frozen vegetables. Simply put those on the grill, and you are ready to go. Grilling is healthier since it allows vegetables to cook more quickly, retaining more nutrients that can keep you well. Don't forget that fish and fruit taste great when grilled; simply put them directly on the grill or cover them loosely in foil. They're delicious. Wrapped in tin foil or placed on top of the grill, this method of cooking vegetables is more nutritionally beneficial than frying or boiling.

3. Meat retains nutrients:

When you cook a slab of meat over an open flame, the riboflavin and thiamine are naturally preserved more. Grilling meat is a better method of preparing it since it retains nutrients such as riboflavin (Vitamin B2) and thiamine (Vitamin B1). Thiamine aids in the degradation of carbohydrates into energy and helps resist certain infections, while Riboflavin aids in energy output. These nutrients are major elements of a balanced diet, and each has a range of health benefits. When food is fried or cooked, minerals and vitamins are lost. Grilling retains more of these nutrients, which enhances the flavor of the meal. The grill can retain moisture, which means you won't need to apply extra condiments to achieve the perfect taste. Consequently, you reduce the consumption of calories and unhealthy foods, which may contribute to obesity.

4. You use less butter:

If you are a grilling master and avoid overcooking your meal, you will have juicy cuts of meat and delicious vegetables. Since the grill retains more moisture, you would be less tempted to add butter or other sauces to your meal. Not only would this suggest you consume fewer calories, yet it often ensures you consume less unhealthy substances.

5. Grilling goes with outside activities:

Grilling takes you outside. Several parents throw a Frisbee or kick a ball across the lawn with their children while grilling dinner. Cooking and dining outside promotes further exercise, which, as we all know, is an additional health benefit to your delightful meal.

6. Grilling aids in weight loss:

It is a fantastic method for cooking vegetables, seafood, and veggie burgers. It is the healthiest way to cook for weight reduction without increasing calorie intake compared to cooking methods such as frying. When the fat melts and runs off the pan, there is less risk of ingesting unwanted fat. This is a significant explanation of why grilling is a healthier method of cooking. All the excess fat is simply poured out, ensuring that it has little risk of causing damage to the core or clogging the arteries. When cooking meat in a frying pan, you must apply additional fat or oil; this fat collects around the meat and is absorbed back into it, eventually ending up in the body. Although grilling does not eliminate fat, it significantly decreases fat consumption.

7. Increased physical activity:

Grilling may be a social event in your backyard for friends or relatives. It is a much more comfortable and healthy way to eat with children playing games and adults socializing and enjoying wine and beer. Everybody is welcome to participate and have a good time. If you have several grills, you will enable many people to grill simultaneously or even host a healthy grilling competition. You might also invite your mates to carry their grills. This is an opportunity for all to make memories and participate in outdoor events.

8. Reduces health risks:

Using grilled foods ensures that you get all of the beneficial vitamins and nutrients they provide. It entails the consumption of fruits, vegetables, and lean meat. This would help you and your family maintain a healthy and fit lifestyle. Additionally, it aids in the reduction of cardiovascular complications such as heart attack, stroke, obesity, hypertension, and even some cancers. Compared to pan-frying, grilled food has less fat and calories. And if you cook foods with low-fat content, they become saturated with fat when they are fried. When meat is grilled, it cooks in its fat. This eliminates the need for more oil, seasonings, or sauce, resulting in decreased calories and fat.

9. Low Sodium Intake:

Are you aware that you might be consuming more sodium than the body requires? This is because at least 70% of our sodium intake comes from restaurants and processed goods. This makes it difficult to maintain a healthy sodium level since the sodium is added before the product is purchased. When food is prepared from scratch and cooked on the grill, the amount of sodium used can be regulated. Grilling enhances the natural flavors, reducing the need for salt.

1.6 Tips for healthy grilling

Before you fire up the grill for tonight's dinner, here are a few ideas to help you make the most of your next meal. Here are some suggestions for improving your family's nutrition when grilling.

1. Buy lean meats:

Though cheeseburgers are a grilling classic, the outdoor menu can be varied. Consider lean cuts of chicken, fish, or pork. Leaner meat is better for you, so when you are in the mood for a sandwich, grab the leanest beef you can find. On the box, look for the code 93/7. This suggests that just 7% of it contains fat.

2. Grill your veggies:

Each meal should include vegetables, so when grilling, toss in some peppers or zucchini. As a side dish, roast sweet corn or prepare veggie kabobs. Another nutrient-dense addition that many people like is a spinach salad with a mild vinaigrette sauce.

3. Use gas rather than charcoal:

According to some doctors, grilling with charcoal can expose a person and the food to cancer-causing chemicals. If you want to cook with charcoal, it is advised that you should not overcook the meat and hold it as far away from the smoke as possible. Doctors suggest using a gas grill whenever possible. Not only is this a more environmentally friendly method of cooking, but you also eliminate the possibility of ingesting a well-known carcinogen.

4. Marinate your meats:

Who doesn't like a steak marinated in some honey garlic glaze or pork chops with lemon pepper? The great news is that marinating not only enhances the flavor of your meal but can also benefit your wellbeing. Some questions about cancer-causing contaminants seep into the meat as it is grilled at elevated temperatures or over charcoal. On the other hand, marinating the beef is believed to further remove up to 99 percent of these contaminants.

5. Try healthy alternatives:

If steak and burgers are your go-to grilling choices, this book is a great source of inspiration. There are countless inventive and unexpected grill recipes. For instance, have you ever attempted to grill a pizza? It is a possibility. To grill something other than beef, pick up some whole-wheat dough from the supermarket, preheat the grill on high, and add some sauce and vegetables.

Although summer is typically associated with grilling, you should also consider an indoor electric grill when the weather cools and the seasons shift. It will tide you over so you can fire up the barbeque.

1.7 Certain foods can never be grilled

As summer draws to a close, you may wish to make the most of the last few days of outdoor grilling. Although grilling enhances the flavor of some foods, certain items cannot be grilled. For various reasons, like protection and flavor, these items should be held away from your grill grates.

1. Bacon:

You will believe the bacon grilled on a grill would be perfectly crisp. Grilling pork, on the other hand, is a health hazard! Grease splatters cannot be placed near the grill blaze due to their flammability. Try cooking the bacon rather than grilling it.

2. Burgers:

Sadly, flipping burgers in the backyard is not the easiest method of preparation. Cast-iron skillets are ideal for preparing burgers.

3. Shrimp Peeled:

Grilling shrimp that are still in their shells is a lot of fun. Grilling the peeled form, on the other hand, is not recommended. Whether marinated or not, shrimp skin is much too susceptible to drying out when subjected to a hot grill.

4. Mignon Filet

Heat fillet mignon in a cast-iron skillet with garlic butter for the finest flavor. Grilling a flank steak is a more secure process.

5. Pork chops:

Although pork chops are resistant to drying out, they are not ideal for grilling.

6. Lettuce with Red and Green Leaves:

Though grilled romaine lettuce is a traditional summer dish, other lettuce varieties should be avoided. Like the red leaf, Boston, and green leaf lettuce, numerous greens retain a significant amount of water and wilt. Additionally, radicchio gets bitterer when cooked.

7. Fish with a Flaky Skin:

You do not want the fish to stick to the grill and flake off before it is ready to eat. Cook the fish on cedar planks to prevent this.

1.8 Some grilling techniques

Here are several tips for a successful and pleasant summer grilling experience.

1: Begin with a thoroughly cleaned grill: Avoid infusing tonight's chicken breasts with the salmon skin from last night's meal. Grates can be cleaned with a robust metal cleaner. (This is better done when the grill is still hot.)

2: Avoid moving the meal: It is preferable to flip the food less often (once is the preferable count for most meats). Allow the meat to cook slightly longer if it becomes stuck to the grill; it can self-unstick when it is time to turn it.

3: Avoid flattening or squeezing meats: A burst of sizzling flame as a result of squeezing a burger with a spatula is very enticing. However, are you aware of what caused the flame to burst? The fat indeed. And are you aware of what fat is? The delicious flavor. Avoid squeezing meat to the point that it loses taste and moisture.

4: Carry a spray bottle in your hand in case of flare-ups: Flames are not the food's best friend; they can char it in an unappealing manner. Have a spray bottle of water in your hand to quickly cool off flare-ups without affecting the heat.

5. Buy a beef thermometer: Unless you are a trained cook, it is difficult to determine meat's temperature merely by handling it. (However, if you are curious, here's how it is done: touch the meat. It is unusual if its tenders, such as the tissue between the index and middle fingers. If it is soft, like your cheek, it is medium-rare; if it is solid, like your forehead, it is well-done.) For most people, a simple temperature check with a thermometer is more accurate. With this inexpensive purchase, your grilling morale will skyrocket.

6: Avoid directly grilling frozen foods: Allowing at least 30 minutes for the meat to come to room temperature before grilling helps even cooking. (However, if you are going for a rare sear — say, if you are grilling tuna, the chilled is fine.)

7: Marginally undercook food items: Carryover cooking happens as food begins to cook until it is taken off the grill. After removing it from the grill, the food's temperature will rise by approximately five degrees, so plan accordingly.

8: Let the meat rest: Enable the meat to rest undisturbed (and unsliced!) for five to fifteen minutes after grilling. This will provide for redistribution of the juices. The longer the pause period, the thicker the meat slice. Resting meat is important for juicy results.

9: Avoid over-charring the meat with bones to ensure complete cooking: Nobody enjoys eating meat that has been coated in black char. Cook bone-in meats with a thicker crust, such as chicken legs or thighs, on high heat for a few minutes before switching to indirect and lower heat on the grill. This would allow the meat to cook more slowly while avoiding an overcooked exterior. Pre-cook the chicken in the oven for 15 to 20 minutes before grilling. Ribs are also ideal for pre-preparation.

10: Keep it simple if you are serving a large group: Managing several cook times for vegetables and various proteins becomes stressful quickly, leading to mistakes and overcooking. Reduce the number of protein options to a minimum and add variety with colorful sauces, side dishes, or condiments.

11. Don't neglect to maintain your grill: Regularly inspect your grease trap and give your grill a good brushing as dirt accumulates. During grill season, check your propane tank for leaks and invest in a good grill cover to keep your grill safe while not in use!

Chapter 2: Grilled Vegetable Recipes

Using more vegetables in my meals is still a pleasure, and summer's bounty makes things much simpler to do. With a hot grill preheated for grilled chicken, pork, or kebabs, you can enjoy slicing up whatever fresh veggies you have on hand and tossing them on the grill for a quick delicious meal for your platter side. Additionally, grilled vegetables make a nutritious vegetarian main dish when diced and added to your favorite vegan pasta salad (with avocado!), or when added to healthy Mediterranean cereal bowls, or when turned into one of my favorite simple grilled veggie sandwiches slathered in ricotta cheese. Grilling extracts the last bit of roasted sweetness from every plain old vegetable, softening and flavoring while imparting a lush, smoky char to each delectably addictive bite. Listed below are some delicious vegetable grilled recipes that can fulfill your appetite.

2.1 Balsamic grilled vegetable

Prep time: 20min

Serves: 10

Ingredients:

- A medium yellow sliced squash
- A medium eggplant, sliced into thick circles
- A medium zucchini
- A red onion, sliced into thick circles

- 1 stemmed, seeded and quartered yellow bell pepper

- 2 peeled and grilled Portobello mushroom caps

- 1 stemmed, seeded and quartered red bell pepper

- 3 green onions

- 2 tbsp. freshly ground black pepper

- 2 tbsp. kosher salt

- ½ cup extra virgin oil

- ½ cup balsamic vinegar

Directions:

- Preheat grill to a high setting.

- To begin, prepare all vegetables. Combine the vegetables, green onions, and mushroom caps in a roasting pan. Season with salt and pepper and mix with balsamic vinegar and olive oil. Cook vegetables, cut side down, for a few minutes on either side or until juicy and nicely marked by the grill.

- Remove from the grill and drizzle with 1/4 cup additional balsamic vinegar. Season to taste with salt and pepper and serve

2.2 Grilled romaine with Balsamic dressing

Prep time: 15min

Serves: 4

Ingredients:

Balsamic dressing:

- ½ cup extra virgin oil

- 3 tbsp. of crumbled Gorgonzola

- 3 tbsp. of balsamic vinegar

- 6 chopped leaves of fresh basil

- 1 tbsp. kosher salt

- 1 chopped garlic clove

- 1 tbsp. of freshly ground pepper

Grilled romaine:

- 2 romaine hearts, cut halved lengthwise
- ¼ cup of crumbled Gorgonzola for garnishing
- 2 tbsp. of canola oil for brushing
- 4 torn leaves of fresh basil for garnishing

Directions:

- To make the balsamic dressing, add the Gorgonzola, olive oil, balsamic vinegar, basil, garlic, a pinch of salt, and a pinch of pepper in a blender. The dressing should be smooth, and the basil and garlic should be finely chopped.
- Preheat a grill pan or grill to medium heat.
- Lightly spray the canola oil onto the cut sides of the romaine. Place the romaine cut-side down on the grill and cook for 1 to 3 minutes, or until grill marks appear and the leaves be slightly charred. Arrange cut-side up on a platter.
- Drizzle the dressing over the romaine. Serve with Gorgonzola and ripped basil.

2.3 Olive garden-style house salad

Prep time: 15min

Serves: 4

Ingredients:

- ¼ cup of extra virgin oil
- 3 tbsp. of Miracle whip
- 2 tbsp. of white wine vinegar
- 1 to 10oz bag American salad blend
- 1 tbsp. of fresh lemon juice
- ¼ tsp. of garlic powder
- 2 tbsp. of grated parmesan cheese
- ½ tsp. of dried Italian seasoning
- ¼ thinly sliced red onion
- 1 small vine-ripened tomato, halved into wedges
- 2 tbsp. of sliced black olives
- 4 pickled peppers or 4 small pepperoncini
- ½ tbsp. of grated parmesan cheese

- ½ cup of large croutons

Directions:

- To make the dressing, in a blender or food processor, combine the garlic, olive oil, Miracle Whip, vinegar, lemon juice, parmesan, Italian seasoning, and 1 to 2 tablespoons water. Puree until fully smooth.

- Prepare the salad: In a big bowl, combine the salad mix with red onion, tomato, pepperoncini, olives, croutons, and cheese. Drizzle with dressing and toss gently.

2.4 Grilled corn on the cob

Prep time: 15min

Serves: 4

Ingredients:

- 4 shucked ears corn, shucked
- 2 tbsp. of butter for serving
- 2 tbsp. of kosher salt

Directions:

- Preheat the grill to high and allow 10 minutes for it to heat up. (Alternatively, preheat the grill pan to the highest setting.) Add some corn and cook, often turning, until corn is fully charred, for around 10 minutes.

- Drizzle warm corn with butter and season with salt.

2.5 Loaded grilled cauliflower

Prep time: 50min

Serves: 4

Ingredients:

- 2 large heads cauliflower
- 1/2 tsp. of garlic powder
- 1/2 tsp. of paprika
- 1/4 cup of extra virgin olive oil
- 2 tbsp. of kosher salt
- 2 cup of shredded cheddar
- 1 tbsp. of freshly ground black pepper

- 8 slices of crumbled cooked bacon
- Some Ranch dressing, for drizzling
- 2 tbsp. of finely chopped chives

Directions:

- Cut the leaves of each cauliflower head, remove them, and then trim the stem to allow the cauliflower to lay flat on the cutting board. (Retain the core!)
- Thinly slice each cauliflower into 3/4" thick "steaks." Some loose florets should be preserved to prepare with the steaks. Whisk together garlic powder, olive oil, and paprika in a small bowl. Season with salt and pepper to taste.
- Preheat a grill or grill pan to a medium temperature. Rub one side of each steak with the olive oil mixture and put it on the grill with the brushed side down. Brush the upper sides with the olive oil mix and cook for around 8 minutes per side, or until soft and both of the sides are charred in spots. Cook until the cheese is melted on top of each cauliflower.
- Toss any remaining florets in the olive oil mix and grill, switching sides often, for around 6 minutes, or until charred and soft.
- Drizzle ranch dressing over cauliflower and top with grilled bacon and chives.

2.6 Grilled Brussels sprouts

Prep time: 30min

Serves: 4

Ingredients:

- 1 lb. of halved Brussels sprouts
- 1/4 cup of balsamic vinegar
- 3 tbsp. of extra virgin olive oil
- 2 tbsp. of kosher salt
- 1 tbsp. of honey
- 2 tsp. of crushed red pepper flakes
- 1 tbsp. of grainy mustard
- 1/2 cup of freshly grated Parmesan, for garnishing

Directions:

- Preheat grill to its highest setting. Combine mustard, Brussels sprouts, vinegar, olive oil, honey, and red pepper flakes in a large mixing bowl and season with salt.

- Using metal skewers, thread sprouts onto them. Grill, turning periodically, for about 10 minutes, or until sprouts are soft and cooked through. Before eating, garnish with Parmesan.

2.7 Best-Ever grilled zucchini

Prep time: 10min

Serves: 2

Ingredients:

- 2 sliced thick strips of medium zucchini

- 1/2 tsp. of lemon zest

- 1 tbsp. of extra virgin olive oil

- 1/4 tsp. of crushed red pepper flakes, some more for garnish

- 2 tbsp. of freshly ground black pepper

- 2 tbsp. of kosher salt

- 4 basil leaves, must be torn into small pieces

Directions:

- Preheat grill to a medium-high temperature. Toss zucchini in a big bowl with oil, red pepper flakes, and lemon zest. Season with some salt and freshly ground pepper.

- Until the grill is warmed, gently brush an oiled paper towel over the grates with tongs.

- Put zucchini on the grill, using tongs. Cook, covered, for 3 minutes. Flip and cook for an additional 2 or 3 minutes on high flame.

- Remove from heat when zucchini is soft and garnish with basil and some red pepper flakes.

2.8 Grilled romaine Caesar wedge

Prep time: 20min

Serves: 4

Ingredients:

- 3/4 cup of mayonnaise

- 1 tsp. of honey mustard

- 1 minced garlic clove

- 1 tsp. of Worcestershire sauce

- 1 tbsp. kosher salt

- Juice of 1/2 lemon

- 1 tbsp. freshly ground black pepper

- 2 tbsp. of extra virgin olive oil

- 1 large quartered head romaine lettuce

- 4 Cooked and chopped slices of bacon

- 3/4 cup of halved grape tomatoes

Directions:

- To make the creamy Caesar dressing, mix mayonnaise, honey mustard, garlic, Worcestershire sauce, and lemon juice in a small cup. Season with some salt and pepper and place aside.

- Preheat a grill pan to a medium-high temperature. Brush romaine wedges with the olive oil and grill for 2 to 3 minutes per side, or until charred and slightly wilted.

- Place romaine on a plate and drizzle with dressing. Serve with bacon and tomatoes on the top.

2.9 Cauliflower and zucchini skewers with feta

Prep time: 20min

Serves: 8

Ingredients:

- 4 large summer squash and zucchini

- 8 skewers, must be soaked in water for 20 minutes

- 1 head cauliflower, cut in florets
- 8 skewers, must be soaked in water for 20 minutes
- 2 tbsp. of extra virgin olive oil, for drizzling
- 1 tbsp. of freshly ground black pepper
- 2 tbsp. of kosher salt
- 1/4 cup of crumbled feta

Directions:

- Preheat grill to a medium-high temperature. Using a Y peeler or mandolin, shave yellow squash and zucchini into long strips. Skewer the Vegetables such as zucchini, yellow squash, and cauliflower. Season with salt and pepper and drizzle with olive oil.
- Grill, occasionally turning, for 10 to 12 minutes, or until vegetables are juicy and slightly charred.
- Crumble the feta and serve.

2.10 Stuffed mini peppers

Prep time: 30min

Serves: 4

Ingredients:

- 4 mini sweet peppers
- 2 cup of goat cheese
- 2 cup cream cheese
- Some herbs

Ingredient notes:

If you are not a fan of goat cheese, feel free to use any herb or garlic cream cheese instead.

Directions:

- The cheese filling should be prepared in advance and refrigerated before ready to fill the peppers. Simply remove it from the refrigerator 30 minutes before filling the peppers to get it to room temperature.
- Prepare the peppers in advance and serve them at room temperature.

- You can also substitute Boursin cheese for the goat cheese and add a squeeze of lemon juice for a simple, flavor-packed filling.

2.11 Balsamic garlic grill mushroom skewers

Prep time: 20min

Serves: 4

Ingredients:

- About 2 pounds of sliced mushrooms, 1/4 inches thick
- 1 tablespoon of tamari or soy sauce
- 2 tablespoons of balsamic vinegar
- 1/2 tsp. of chopped thyme
- 1 tsp. of salt
- 3 cloves of chopped garlic
- 1 tbsp. of pepper

Directions:

- Marinate the mushrooms for 30 minutes in a mixture of all ingredients.
- Skewer the mushrooms and grill them over medium to high heat for around 2 to 3 minutes per side, or until only soft and slightly charred.

2.12 Grilled vegetable kabobs with fajita butter

Prep time: 30min

Serves: 4

Ingredients:

- 5 ears of fresh corn
- A large red bell pepper
- 3 zucchini
- A large red onion

- 8 ounces of mushrooms
- 8oz small Brussels sprouts
- 1/2 cup of salted butter
- 2 tablespoons of fresh lemon juice
- 1 packet of **Old el Paso fajita seasoning mix**
- 12 **thick** metal skewers **or wooden skewers**

Directions:

- If using wooden skewers, soak them in water for at least 30 minutes before cooking. Preheat the grill to medium-low heat, around 325 degrees F.
- Shuck the corn and cut it into 1 1/2 rounds. Cut the zucchini into 1-inch rounds. Cut the onions and bell pepper into 1.5 inch square pieces, and discard the pepper seeds. Trim the Brussels sprouts and thread the vegetables onto the skewers in an alternate pattern.
- Melt the butter and whisk with the Old El Paso Fajita Seasoning Mix and lemon juice.
- If using metal skewers: grill for 15 minutes, dry. Then brush with the fajita butter and grill for another 5 minutes. Rotate the skewers every 3-5 minutes. Brush the remaining fajita butter over the skewers once off the grill.
- If using wooden skewers: Grill the skewers dry for 20 minutes, rotating them every 3-5 minutes. Then remove the skewers from the heat and brush thoroughly with fajita butter. Serve warm!

2.13 Grilled vegetables with basil vinaigrette

Prep time: 30min

Serves: 4

Ingredients:

Vegetables:

- 1 medium trimmed and sliced zucchini
- 1 large seeded and sliced red bell pepper
- 1 trimmed and sliced medium yellow squash
- 1 large seeded and sliced yellow bell pepper
- About 2 cups of cauliflower florets or broccoli florets

- About 6 cores removed baby Portobello mushrooms
- 1/2 teaspoon of salt or to taste
- 1 tablespoon of olive oil
- 1/2 teaspoon of freshly ground black pepper or to taste

Basil vinaigrette:

- About 2 cups of loosely packed fresh basil leaves, about 2oz or about 2 large handfuls
- Half of a large shallot about the size of 2 garlic cloves
- About 1/3 cup of olive oil
- 1/2 teaspoon of freshly ground black pepper or to taste
- 2 tablespoons of rice wine vinegar, apple cider or your favorite vinegar
- 1/2 teaspoon of salt or to taste
- 1 tablespoon of honey or agave or to taste
- Splash water, optional

Directions:

- **Vegetables:** Preheat a gas grill to medium-high heat or brush a grill pan with a nonstick grill spray.
- Combine the oil, vegetables, salt, and pepper in a big bowl and toss to cover uniformly.
- Arrange vegetables in a single layer on the grill and cook for approximately 5 minutes on the first side, then flip and cook for approximately 5 minutes on the second side, or until vegetables are cooked through, juicy, and as blackened as needed. All vegetables, grills, and personal preferences for blackening could vary; cook until the desired doneness is achieved depending on your variables. Now, remove the vegetables from the grill and set them aside.
- **Basil Vinaigrette:** Combine all ingredients except the water in the canister of a high-speed blender or food processor and mix at high speed until smooth.

2.14 Marinated grilled vegetables with avocado whipped feta

Prep time: 1 hour

Serves: 4

Ingredients:

- 1/4 cup of olive oil

- 1 tablespoon of brown sugar

- 2 tablespoons of low-sodium soy sauce

- 4 minced garlic cloves

- 1/2 teaspoon of pepper

- 2 zucchini squash, must be sliced into rounds

- 1 teaspoon of smoked paprika

- 2 large sliced Portobello mushroom caps

- 1 large sliced eggplant

- 2 sliced bell peppers

- 1 large onion must be sliced into rounds

- 2 medium sweet potatoes

- 1 baguette, must be sliced into rounds

- 1 cup halved radishes

- a handful of fresh oregano, rosemary , basil, and thyme for garnish

Avocado whipped feta:

- 8 ounces of feta cheese, must be crumbled and at room temperature

- 1 cubed avocado

- 1 tablespoon of olive oil

Directions:

- Whisk together the oil, paprika, brown sugar, soy sauce, garlic, and pepper in a medium bowl. In a big baking dish, arrange the zucchini, onion, mushrooms, eggplant, and radish slices. Cover the dish with the marinade and chill for at least 30 minutes. Meanwhile, parboil the sweet potato so that it has the right consistency when grilled. Place the slices in a saucepan with enough water to cover them and bring to a boil, boiling for approximately 1 to 2 minutes. Then take them out and toss them in the marinade!

- Preheat the grill to the maximum possible temperature. Brush both sides of the baguette with olive oil.

- When the grill is heated, use tongs to remove the vegetables from the marinade and put them on the grill. Start grilling the peppers, potatoes, and eggplant. If your zucchini and radishes are small, you may either use a grill plate or cover them in aluminum foil. You should grill until the desired level of char is achieved or until grill marks emerge and the vegetables are golden.

- You can grill your bread second since it tends to burn easily. Arrange the vegetables and bread on a baking sheet or platter. Season with salt and pepper to taste. Sprinkle fresh herbs over the vegetables. Serve directly with the avocado feta.

Avocado whipped feta:

- In a food processor, add all of the crumbled feta and spin until little crumbs remain. Puree the avocado for about 4-5 minutes, scraping the sides as required, until the feta is pure creamy. Serve with a sprinkle of additional herbs and feta crumbs on top.

2.15 Grilled vegetable platter

Prep time: 20min and marinating grill: 10min

Serves: 6

Ingredients:

- 1/4 cup of olive oil
- 4 teaspoons of balsamic vinegar
- 2 tablespoons of honey
- A medium yellow summer squash
- 1 teaspoon of dried oregano
- 1/8 teaspoon of pepper
- 1/2 teaspoon of garlic powder
- 2 tbsp. dash salt
- 3 small carrots, must be cut in half lengthwise
- 1 pound trimmed fresh asparagus
- A large sweet red pepper
- A medium red onion, must be cut into wedges

Directions:

- Mix together all the ingredients in a shallow bowl. In a large bowl, add 3 tablespoons marinade. Add vegetables to the coat. Cover and marinate at room temperature for 1-1/2 hours.

- Transfer the Vegetables to a grilling grid, and place them on the grill rack. Grill vegetables, wrapped, over medium heat for 8-12 minutes, or until crisp-tender, turning periodically.

- Arrange vegetables in a single layer on a large serving tray. Drizzle leftover marinade on the top and serve.

2.16 Grilled watermelon

Prep Time: 15 minutes

Serves: 6

Ingredients:

- ½ cup of diced red onion
- 1 minced garlic clove
- 1½ cups of raw corn kernels
- teaspoons of Tabasco Green Sauce
- Heaping ¼ teaspoon of sea salt
- 6 1.5-inch of watermelon wedges
- Some cooking spray, for grill
- ½ cup of crumbled feta cheese
- ½ cup of diced red bell pepper
- Basil and mint leaves
- Lime wedges, optional
- 1 diced small avocado

Directions:

- Preheat the grill to medium-high flame.
- Combine the corn, red pepper, onion, salt, garlic, and Tabasco Green Sauce in a medium mixing bowl. Refrigerate until ready.
- Gently brush the grill grates with some cooking spray. Grill the watermelon for 2 to 3 minutes on each side or until char marks appear on it.
- Remove them from the grill and set aside to cool for a few minutes before topping with the corn mixture, feta, avocado, and fresh herbs. If you like, serve with extra lime wedges or tabasco and on the side.

2.17 Grilled Asparagus

Prep Time: 5 minutes

Serves: 4

Ingredients

- 2 tbsp. of extra virgin olive oil
- 2 tbsp. of freshly ground black pepper
- 2 lb. of asparagus, stalks trimmed
- 2 tbsp. of kosher salt

Directions:

- Over a high flame, prepare a grill or grill pan. Season asparagus generously with some pepper and salt after gently tossing it in oil.
- Grill it for 3 to 4 minutes, frequently rotating, until tender and charred.

2.18 Grilled Green Beans

Prep Time: 10 minutes

Serves: 4

Ingredients

- tbsp. of extra virgin olive oil
- 2 tbsp. of soy sauce
- 2 tsp. of honey
- 1 lb. of green beans, ends trimmed
- 2 tbsp. Sesame seeds, for garnishing
- Chopped roasted peanuts, (optional)
- 1 tbsp. of chili garlic paste
- A pinch red pepper flakes
- 2 tbsp. of kosher salt
- A cup thinly sliced green onions, for garnishing

Directions:

- Preheat the grill pan to medium-high heat. Whisk together the oil, paste, honey, chili garlic, soy sauce, and red pepper flakes in a large bowl, then add the green beans and toss it to cover. Season with some salt.

- Put green beans on the grill pan and cook for about 7 minutes, or until charred all over. (If you are using a grill, cover the grates with a thick piece of foil and put green beans on the top.)

- Toss with sesame seeds, green onions, and peanuts before serving.

2.19 Grilled Eggplant

Prep Time: 15 minutes

Serves: 4

Ingredients

Grilled eggplant:

- 2 tbsp. of **extra virgin olive oil**, for drizzling
- 2 medium eggplants, sliced into ¼-inch thick circles
- 2 tbsp. sea salt

Couscous salad topping:

- ½ teaspoon of **extra-virgin olive oil**, and some more for drizzling
- 1/2 teaspoon of zest
- ½ cup of dry Israeli couscous
- 1 grated garlic clove
- 1 tablespoon of lemon juice
- tablespoons of chopped dried dates or apricots
- heaping 1/4 teaspoon of sea salt
- 2 tbsp. of freshly ground black pepper
- Pinches red pepper flakes
- ¼ cup of mint leaves, for garnishing
- ¼ cup of finely chopped parsley
- tablespoons of sliced or chopped almonds

Directions:

- Start by making the couscous salad. Cook the couscous in a pot of salted boiling water, for around 7 to 8 minutes. Drain and put in a medium mixing pan. Add the salt, lemon juice, pepper, garlic, lemon zest, dried apricots, and red pepper flakes to the olive oil mixture. Season after adding the parsley and almonds.

- Cook the eggplant on the grill. Preheat the grill to medium-high. Drizzle olive oil over the eggplant and season with some salt and pepper. Grill for 2 to 3 minutes on each side, or until well-charred and soft.

- Place the eggplant on a platter with the couscous salad on top. Serve with some fresh mint as a garnish. Drizzle with some olive oil and season to taste. T can serves four people as a side dish or two people as a main course.

2.20 Grilled Ratatouille Tar tines

Prep Time: 5 minutes

Serves: 4

Ingredients

- 1 eggplant of medium size, sliced into ¼-inch thick circles
- whole scallions
- 1 zucchini, sliced lengthwise in half
- 1 red bell pepper, halved, ribs and seeds removed
- 1 cup cherry tomatoes, halved
- 1 tbsp. of extra virgin olive oil, for drizzling
- 1 tbsp. of sea salt
- 1 teaspoon of sherry vinegar
- ¼ cup of fresh chopped basil
- 1 minced garlic clove
- 1 cup of goat cheese or hummus
- 1 teaspoon of herbs de Provence

- 8 slices of toasted bread

Directions:

- Preheat the grill pan or grill to medium-high flame.
- Drizzle olive oil and a sprinkle of salt over the eggplant, zucchini, red pepper, and scallions. Grill for about 3 minutes each side before charred.
- Take the vegetables off from the grill, set them aside to cool slowly, and then cut them into 1-inch bits. Toss them with garlic, cherry tomatoes, herbs de Provence, sherry vinegar, and basil in a large dish.
- Season to taste, then serve with a spread of hummus or goat cheese on toasted bread.

2.21 Grilled fava beans with mint, lemon zest and sumac

Prep Time: 15 minutes

Serves: 4

Ingredients

- 1 tbsp. of olive oil to coat
- 1 tbsp. of salt
- 20–30 fresh Fava beans (in the pod)

Dressing:

- 1 finely minced garlic clove
- 1 tablespoon of finely chopped shallot (optional)
- tablespoons of **olive oil**
- zest from one medium lemon
- 1/2 teaspoon of **salt**
- 1 teaspoon of sumac

Garnish:

- 1/4 cup of Italian Parsley
- 1/2 teaspoon of Aleppo chili or normal chili flakes (optional)
- 1/4 cup chopped of fresh mint

- squeeze of a lemon, optional

Directions:

- Preheat the grill to medium-high temperature.
- Toss the fava beans in a small amount of olive oil, just enough to cover them, then season generously with some salt.
- Cover the grill and cook each side before deep grill marks emerge (about 4-5 minutes per side). Make sure that the inner bean is soft with a tester.
- Put them on a platter and top with dressing. Sprinkle with parsley and fresh mint, and Aleppo chili flakes.
- Top with a squeeze of lemon if you want them to have a better lemon taste.

2.22 Grilled Portobello bruschetta mushrooms

Prep Time: 10 minutes

Serves: 6

Ingredients

- tablespoons of finely chopped red onion
- tablespoons divided, shredded fresh basil
- 2 cups of halved cherry or grape tomatoes
- tablespoons of **Garlic Butter**
- large Portobello Mushrooms, washes and dried, stems removed
- Salt and pepper for taste
- 1 teaspoon of dried oregano

Balsamic glaze:

- 2 teaspoons of brown sugar (optional)
- 1/4 cup of balsamic vinegar

Directions:

- Preheat the grill plates, grill pan, over medium heat. Cooking oil should be lightly greased on grill surfaces.
- In a medium-sized mixing dish, add the red onion, tomatoes, and 2 teaspoons of fresh basil, salt, and pepper. Mix, so it is well combined and then set aside.

- In a shallow saucepan (or microwave-safe bowl), melt the oregano and garlic butter together until garlic smell appears. Brush both sides of each mushroom with garlic butter.

- Grill for 5 minutes or until the vegetables are only begin to soften.

- Drizzle the balsamic glaze over the mushrooms and the tomato/basil mixture. To eat, season with a pinch of salt and garnish with the basil leaves.

Balsamic glaze:

- Prepare it while mushrooms are grilling, if making from scratch. In a small saucepan over high flame, mix the sugar and vinegar and bring to a boil. Reduce to low heat and cook for 5-8 minutes, or until the mixture has thickened and condensed to a glaze. (If you don't want to use sugar, let it reduce for about 12-15 minutes on low heat.)

For the Oven:

- Preheat the oven to high grill or broil settings. Place the oven shelf in the center of the oven. Prepare the mushrooms with garlic butter according to the directions mentioned above. Put them on a baking tray, buttered side down. Grill or broil the mushrooms for around 8 minutes or before they begin to turn lightly brown.

Continue with the directions above once the chicken is cooked through.

Chapter: 3 Grilled Meat Recipes

For many, grilled meat is the classic illustration of what makes outdoor cooking so wonderful—but word has spread, and people are discovering all kinds of foods that benefit from certain times over the coals (or the gas flames). Grilled pizzas, grilled salads, grilled cheese, grilled cakes, grilled fish, and grilled beer-can cabbage are all grilled to perfection. However, even though grilled meat is sharing the spotlight, it still has a part to play. If it is beef, pork, or lamb, this chapter has compiled a list of your favorite grilled meat recipes that you can enjoy during the summer.

3.1 Jerk chicken

Prep time: 2 hours 40min

Serves: 4

Ingredients:

Chicken:

- A bunch of green onions and some thinly sliced for garnishing
- 1 roughly chopped jalapeno
- 2 cloves of garlic
- 8 pieces of bone-in chicken thighs or drumsticks
- Juice of a lime
- 1 tbsp. of packed brown sugar

- 2 tbsp. of extra virgin oil

- 1 ½ tbsp. of ground allspices

- ½ tsp. ground cinnamon

- 1 tsp. of dried thyme

- 2 tbsp. kosher salt

Directions:

- In a blender, add the green onions, garlic, one teaspoon salt, jalapeno, lime juice, oil, allspice, thyme, brown sugar, cinnamon, and two tablespoons water until smooth. Set aside 1/4 cup.

- Season chicken with salt and pepper in a shallow dish.

- Pour the remainder of the marinade over the chicken and flip to cover. Allow at least 2 hours or up to overnight to marinate in the refrigerator, turning once or twice. 3.

- When it is ready to grill, preheat grill to medium-high and oil grates. Grill chicken, turning periodically, for about 10 minutes, or until charred in spots.

- Move chicken to a cooler area of the grill and brush chicken with reserved marinade. Grill, wrapped, for a further 10 to 15 minutes or until chicken is cooked through.

3.2 Honey soy grilled Pork chops

Prep time: 55 min

Serves: 4

Ingredients:

- 2 tbsp. red pepper flakes

- ¼ cup of honey

- 2 minced garlic cloves

- ½ cup of low-sodium soy sauce

- 4 boneless pork chops

Directions:

- In a large mixing bowl, combine honey, garlic, red pepper flakes and soy sauce.

   Add the pork chops and cover them and refrigerate for approximately 30 minutes or up to 2 hours.

- Preheat grill to medium-high heat and cook for 8 minutes per side, or until seared and cooked through. Allow it to rest for 5min before serving.

3.3 California grilled chicken

Prep time: 50min

Serves: 4

Ingredients:

- ¾ cup of balsamic vinegar
- 2 tbsp. of honey
- 1 tsp. garlic powder
- 2 tbsp. of extra-virgin olive oil
- 2 sliced tomatoes
- 1 tsp. of kosher salt
- 2 tsp. of Italian seasoning
- 1 tbsp. freshly ground black pepper
- 4 slices of mozzarella cheese
- 2 skinless and boneless chicken breasts
- 4 slices of avocado
- 2 tbsp. of freshly sliced basil for garnishing
- Some Balsamic glaze for drizzling

Directions:

- Stir together garlic powder, balsamic vinegar, oil, honey, and Italian seasoning in a small bowl. Season with some salt and pepper. Pour evenly over chicken and marinate for 20 minutes.
- Preheat grill to medium-high when ready to grill. Oil the grates and chicken should be grilled until crispy and cooked through, for around 8 minutes per side.
- Place avocado, mozzarella, and tomato on top of the chicken and cover grill for 2 minutes to melt.
- Sprinkle basil on top and drizzle some balsamic glaze.

3.4 Philly cheesesteak foil packs

Prep time: 25min

Serves: 4

Ingredients:

- 1 lb. thinly sliced flank steak
- ½ thinly sliced onion
- 2 thinly sliced bell peppers
- 2 minced garlic cloves
- 2 tbsp. of extra virgin oil
- 2 tbsp. of Italian seasoning
- 1 tbsp. of kosher salt
- 4 slices of provolone
- 1 tbsp. of freshly ground black pepper
- Some chopped fresh parsley for garnishing

Directions:

- Preheat grill to a medium-high temperature. Toss steak, Italian seasoning, peppers, garlic, onion, and olive oil in a large bowl. Season with some salt and pepper.
- Place the steak mixture in the foil packets. Fold up the packets and grill for about 10min.
- Open packages, sprinkle with provolone and cover the grill for 2 minutes to melt.
- Serve with garnished parsley.

3.5 Broccoli and beef kebabs

Prep time: 35min

Serves: 4

Ingredients:

- 1/3 cup of low-sodium soy sauce
- Juice or 1 large or 2 limes and some juice for serving
- ¼ cup brown sugar
- 1 tbsp. of ground ginger
- 2 cups of broccoli florets
- 1 lb. sirloin steak cut into cubes

- 2 tbsp. of freshly ground black pepper

- 2 tbsp. of extra virgin oil

- Some green onions for garnishing

Directions:

- Preheat grill to a medium-high temperature. Whisk together brown sugar, soy sauce, lime juice, and ginger in a small bowl. Add in steak until evenly coated. Allow at least 15 minutes and up to 2 hours for marinating in the refrigerator.

- In a separate bowl, combine broccoli florets and olive oil.

- Arrange steak and broccoli onto skewers and season lightly with pepper.

- Grill, occasionally turning, for 8 minutes, or until steak is cooked through.

- Squeeze lime over the top and garnish some green onions and serve.

3.6 Peppers and sausage foil pack

Prep time: 30min

Serves: 4

Ingredients:

- 8 Italian sausage line

- 2 thinly sliced large onions

- 4 thinly chopped bell peppers

- ¼ cup extra virgin oil, divide in half

- 1 tbsp. of freshly ground black pepper

- 1 tbsp. of kosher salt

- Some chopped fresh parsley for garnishing

Directions:

- Preheat the grill to its highest temperature. Cut four 12" long sheets of aluminum.

- Grill sausages for 3 minutes per side until charred, then divide among foil. Season with salt and pepper and arrange peppers and onions on top. Drizzle each with one tablespoon of olive oil.

- Crosswise fold the foil packages over the pepper and sausage mixture to completely enclose the food. Seal the top and bottom edges by rolling them together.

- Grill for 13 to 15 minutes, or until onions and peppers are soft, and sausage is cooked.
- Garnish with some parsley and serve.

3.7 Caprese steak

Prep time: 30min

Serves: 4

Ingredients:

- ¾ cup of balsamic vinegar
- 2 tbsp. of honey
- 3 minced garlic cloves
- 2 tbsp. of extra virgin oil
- 1 tbsp. of dried oregano
- 1 tbsp. of dried thyme
- 4 large pieces of sirloin or 4 6oz filet mignon
- 1 tbsp. of kosher salt
- 2 sliced beefsteak tomatoes
- 4 slices of mozzarella cheese
- Some fresh basil leaves for serving

Directions:

- Whisk together the balsamic vinegar, olive oil, dried thyme, garlic, honey, and dried oregano in a small bowl.
- Pour over steak and set aside for 20 minutes to marinate.
- Season tomatoes with sea salt and freshly ground pepper.
- Preheat the grill to a high temperature. Grill steaks for 4 to 5 minutes on each side, top with some mozzarella and tomatoes, cover the grill for 2 minutes, or until cheese is melted.
- Garnish with basil just before serving.

3.8 BBQ chicken with sweet chili peach glaze

Prep time: 40min

Serves: 4

Ingredients:

- Pitted and divides slices of 5 peaches
- Zest and juice of a lime
- ½ cup of sweet chili sauce
- 8 green onions
- 2 red onions, sliced into ¾ inch rings
- Bamboo skewers, must be soaked in water
- 2 tbsp. of extra virgin oil for drizzling
- 1 tbsp. of freshly ground black pepper
- 1 tbsp. of kosher salt
- 2 lb. skin-on and bone-in chicken thighs

Directions:

- Add 1 roughly chopped peach, lime juice, sweet chili sauce, and lime zest in a blender and then pulse and blend until it gets smooth, then move to a small bowl. Arrange remaining peaches cut side up with some green onions on a rimmed sheet pan. Skewer onions through the middle and arrange on a sheet pan. Drizzle with olive oil and toss to coat. Season with sea salt and freshly ground pepper.

- Preheat the grill to a medium-high temperature. Meanwhile, clean chicken thoroughly and pat dry fully. Arrange chicken on a separate rimmed sheet pan and drizzle with some olive oil, and season with salt and pepper.

- Place the chicken on the grill and cook for 10 minutes, and cover it. Cook chicken on each side and add green onions, peaches, and onions to the grill. After 5 minutes, remove the cover and flip the vegetables and peaches. Brush glaze on chicken as it hits an internal temperature of 150 to 155°. Turn the chicken over and continue cooking until all sides are glazed and browned and the internal temperature reaches 165°; the total cooking time for the chicken is approximately 25 minutes. Vegetables and peaches should have dark grill marks and a mild burnt appearance; cooking time should be about 8 and 10 minutes.

- Transfer them to a large platter and drizzle the remaining glaze over the top and serve.

3.9 Barbecue chicken with chili lime corn on the cob

Prep time: 50min

Serves: 4

Ingredients:

- 2 skin-on and bone-in chicken breast
- 2 tbsp. freshly ground black pepper
- 2 skin-on and bone-in chicken thighs and legs (connected)
- 2 cups of barbeque sauce (homemade or store-bought)
- 1 tbsp. of grated lime zest
- 1 tsp. of chili powder
- ½ cup of Country crock original
- 4 husks removed ears corn
- ½ tsp. of cumin
- Some lime wedges for serving

Directions:

- Preheat grill to high heat. Season chicken with some salt and pepper and grill, turning once, for 15 minutes, until nicely charred. Reduce heat to medium-low and baste the chicken with one cup barbecue sauce. Cover and continue grilling for an additional 15 minutes, then baste with the remaining one cup barbecue sauce. Cover and continue grilling for a further 15 minutes, or until the internal temperature hits 165°.

- Meanwhile, whisk together lime juice and zest, Country Crock Original, chili powder, and cumin in a small bowl. Season with salt and pepper to taste.

- About 15 minutes until the chicken is done, rub half of the chili-lime spread over the corn and season with some salt and pepper. Cover and cook, frequently turning, for 15 minutes, or until soft and slightly charred.

- Dollop additional chili-lime spread on corn and serve with lime and barbecue chicken.

3.10 Shortcut BBQ ribs

Prep time: 40min

Serves: 4

Ingredients:

- 1 rack baby back ribs of about 3 lbs.

- 4 minced garlic cloves

- 1 tbsp. of kosher salt

- 3 tbsp. of brown sugar

- Some freshly ground black pepper

- 2 tbsp. of smoked paprika

- 1 cup of barbecue sauce

Directions:

- Preheat the grill or the grill pan to moderately high heat. Cut the ribs into three parts.

- In a large saucepan over medium heat, place ribs and add enough water to cover. Add approximately 1 tablespoon salt, carry to a boil, and simmer to low heat for 20 minutes. Drain the ribs and place them on a sheet tray. Using paper towels, thoroughly dry the ribs.

- In the meantime, prepare the spice rub. In a small bowl, combine garlic, paprika, brown sugar, 1 teaspoon cinnamon, and 1/2 teaspoon black pepper. Spoon the paste onto the ribs and rub with your hands all over.

- Cook ribs for about 10 minutes, turning halfway through, on a grill or grill pan. Brush barbecue sauce over ribs and continue cooking for an additional 1 minute, or until finely charred. Serve the ribs with barbeque sauce.

3.11 Grilled skirt steak with blistered guacamole and tomatoes

Prep time: 50min

Serves: 4

Ingredients:

- 1 ½ lb. skirt steak

- 1 tsp. of coriander

- 2 tsp. of cumin

- 2 minced garlic cloves

- 3 tbsp. of extra virgin oil, divided in half

- 4 tbsp. of lime juice

- 3 diced avocados

- 2 tbsp. of finely chopped fresh cilantro, and some cilantro leaves for garnishing

- 2 tbsp. of finely chopped red onion
- ½ tsp. of crushed red pepper flakes
- ¾ cup halved yellow grape tomatoes
- ¾ cup halved red grape tomatoes
- 1 tbsp. of freshly ground black pepper
- 1 tbsp. of kosher salt

Directions:

- In a deep glass baking dish, place the steak. Whisk together in a small bowl Cumin, garlic, coriander, 2 teaspoons lime juice, and 2 tsp. oil. Marinate steak for 10 minutes by pouring the mixture over it and turning to coat.

- Prepare the guacamole: Mash avocado, cilantro, onion, red pepper flakes, and remaining 1/2 tbsp. lime juice together in a medium bowl until chunky, then season with some salt.

- Season tomatoes with salt and pepper in a medium bowl. Mix tomatoes with leftover 1 tablespoon olive oil.

- Preheat a grill pan to a medium-high temperature. Grill tomatoes for 4 minutes or until blistered, then remove and raise heat to high.

- Season steak with salt and pepper and place on grill. Grill 3 minutes per side at medium heat, then let it sit for 5 minutes.

- Against the grain, thinly slice the steak. Serve with cilantro and blistered tomatoes on top and guacamole on the side.

3.12 Rosemary garlic burgers with gruyere

Prep time: 50min

Serves: 4

Ingredients:

- 1 tbsp. of extra-virgin olive oil
- 1 tbsp. of brown sugar
- 1 large red onion, cut in half moons
- 1 tbsp. of balsamic vinegar
- 1 tbsp. of kosher salt
- 1/4 cup of red wine

- 1/4 cup of grainy Dijon mustard

- 1 tbsp. of freshly ground black pepper

- 1 minced garlic clove

- 1 1/4 lb. of ground beef

- 1 tbsp. of finely chopped fresh rosemary

- 4 potato hamburger buns or any other hamburger buns

- 3oz. of thinly sliced Gruyere

- A Tomato for serving

- Some lettuce for serving.

Directions:

- Heat oil in a big sauté pan on medium-high heat. Add onions and cook for 4 minutes, or before they begin to soften. Cook for an additional 3 minutes, stirring in balsamic vinegar and brown sugar. Allow wine to evaporate for 2 to 3 minutes before seasoning with salt and pepper.

- Preheat the broiler to the hottest temperature.

- Mix garlic, ground beef, and rosemary in a big bowl and season well with salt and black pepper. In your hands, carefully combine the mixture and form it into four patties. Season all sides of the patties with salt and pepper.

- Preheat a finely oiled grill pan on high heat and cook for 3 minutes, flipping halfway through. Cook for an extra 3 minutes before adding the Gruyere to the burgers. Transfer pan to broiler and broil for 15 to 30 seconds, or until cheese is melted.

- Spread 1 tablespoon of Dijon mustard on the bottom of each bun. Top with balsamic-glazed onions, burgers, and bun tops and serve with tomato and lettuce

3.13 Steak fajita skewers

Prep time: 5omin

Serves: 8

Ingredients:

- 1 lb. of sirloin steak, cut in large cubes

- 1 pack of small flour tortilla, must be torn into large pieces

- 1 bunch of scallions, cut into thirds

- 1 tbsp. of kosher salt

- 4 big bell peppers, cut in large pieces

- 1 tbsp. of extra virgin olive oil, for drizzling

- 8 skewers, must be soaked in water for about 20min

- 1 tbsp. of freshly ground black pepper

Directions:

- Preheat grill to a medium-high temperature. Using skewers, thread steak, scallions, rolled tortillas, and peppers. Season with pepper and salt and drizzle with olive oil.

- Grill, occasionally turning, for around 7 minutes, or until steak is medium-rare and veggies are juicy and slightly charred.

3.14 Grilled chicken with Greek salad pita pockets

Prep time: 25min

Serves: 4

Ingredients:

- 1 lb. of chicken breast cutlets

- 6 tbsp. of extra-virgin olive oil, divide in half

- 2 tbsp. Juice of 1/2 lemon

- 1 tsp. of dried oregano

- 1 tbsp. of kosher salt

- 3 minced small garlic cloves

- 1 tbsp. of Black pepper

- 1/2 cup of red grape tomatoes, cut in lengthwise

- ½ cup of yellow grape tomatoes, cut in lengthwise

- 2 tbsp. of red wine vinegar

- ¼ cup of pitted kalamata olives cut in half

- ½ thinly sliced red onion cut into half moons

- 1/4 cup of chopped parsley or fresh mint

- 1/2 cup crumbled feta

- 4 halved and lightly toasted whole-wheat pitas

Directions:

- In a small baking dish, place chicken cutlets. Whisk together lemon juice, 2 teaspoons olive oil, oregano, and 2 garlic cloves in a small bowl. Distribute mixture evenly over chicken cutlets and marinate for 10 minutes.

- Preheat the grill pan to high heat. Remove cutlets from marinade and season with salt and pepper on both sides. Grill until well cooked, around 3 minutes per side. Allow it to sit for 5 minutes before slicing thinly.

- Toss cucumber, red onion, tomatoes, feta, and mint in a large bowl (and olives, if using). Whisk together the red wine vinegar and the remaining garlic clove in a small bowl. Slowly whisk in the remaining 4 teaspoons of olive oil in a steady stream. Season with salt and freshly ground pepper. Drizzle vinaigrette over the salad and gently toss to combine.

- Stuff each half of the pita pocket with grilled chicken and garnish with Greek salad.

3.15 Italian chicken skewers

Prep time: 25min

Serves: 8

Ingredients:

- 1 lb. of boneless and skinless chicken breasts, cut in large cubes

- 1 tbsp. freshly ground black pepper

- 1 tbsp. of kosher salt

- 2 tbsp. of tomato paste

- 3 minced garlic cloves, minced

- 1/4 cup of extra virgin olive oil and some more for drizzling

- 8 skewers, must be soaked in water for about 20 minutes

- 1 tbsp. of chopped fresh Italian parsley and some more leaves for garnish

- 1 baguette French bread, cut in cubes

Directions:

- Season the chicken with some pepper and salt. In a large bowl, add tomato paste, garlic cloves, olive oil, and some chopped parsley. Toss in chicken and coat properly. Place it for 30 minutes in the refrigerator.

- Preheat the grill to a medium-high temperature. Skewer the chicken and bread. Season with pepper and salt and drizzle with olive oil.

- Grill, turning periodically, for about 10 minutes, or until meat is cooked through and bread is mildly charred. Garnish with parsley if you desire.

3.16 Spicy cucumber salad with grilled Korean flank steak

Prep time: 40min

Serves: 4

Ingredients:

- 1 tbsp. of low-sodium soy sauce
- 1/2 cup of rice wine vinegar, divide in half
- 2 tbsp. of vegetable oil
- 4 minced cloves garlic
- 2 tbsp. of honey
- 2 tbsp. of freshly minced ginger
- 3 tbsp. of sesame oil, divide in half
- 1 1/2 lb. of flank steak
- 1 tsp. of sugar
- 3 tbsp. of Sriracha, divide in half
- 1 tsp. of crushed red pepper flakes
- 1 tbsp. of kosher salt

- 2 seeded and thinly sliced large cucumbers, cut into lengthwise
- Some cooked white rice for serving
- Some sliced green onions for serving

Directions:

- Bring 2 cups of water and rice to a boil in a saucepan, then reduce to low heat and cover and simmer for 15 minutes. Take the saucepan off the heat and set it aside, covered, before ready to use. Season with salt and fluff with a fork. You may sprinkle Sesame seeds on top.
- Add 12 cup soy sauce, half the rice wine vinegar, vegetable oil, garlic, honey, ginger, 2 tablespoons sesame oil, and 2 tablespoons Sriracha in a large mixing bowl. Pour half of the sauce over the flank steak, marinate for 10 minutes, and reserve the remaining sauce.
- To make the cucumber salad, mix together the remaining rice wine vinegar, Sriracha, soy sauce, sesame sugar, oil, and red pepper flakes in another large bowl. Season with salt and pepper after adding the cucumber.
- Preheat a grill or grill pan to a high temperature. Season steak with some salt and pepper and grill for about 5 to 6 minutes on each side for medium-rare. Transfer to a cutting board and allow to cool for 5 minutes before slicing thinly across the grain. Combine juices in a shallow bowl with the remaining sauce.
- Drizzle sauce over steak and top with scallions. Serve with rice and cucumber salad.

3.17 Grilled chicken with kale Caesar salad

Prep time: 25min

Serves: 4

Ingredients:

- 1/4 cup of freshly grated Parmesan cheese, plus more for serving
- Juice of 3 lemons, divide in half
- 1/4 cup of 2% Greek yogurt
- 2 anchovy fillets
- 1 minced garlic clove
- 1/2 tsp. of Worcestershire sauce
- 3 tbsp. of extra virgin olive oil, divide in half

- 1 tbsp. of freshly ground black pepper

- 1 tbsp. of kosher salt

- 1 cleaned and thinly sliced large bunch of Tuscan kale

- 4 to 5-oz. of chicken breasts

- 1/2 cup of red grape tomatoes

Directions:

- Mix Parmesan, Greek yogurt, 1/4 cup lemon juice, Worcestershire sauce, anchovy paste or anchovies, and garlic in a mini food processor and pulse. Add 2 teaspoons olive oil and puree till smooth when the motor is running. Season with salt and freshly ground pepper.

- Preheat a grill pan or grill to a high temperature. Chicken should be seasoned with some salt and pepper and rubbed with olive oil. Grill until it turns golden and cooked through, for around 7 to 8 minutes per side, then brush chicken breasts with remaining lemon juice and move to a cutting board. Allow it to rest for 5 minutes before slicing into thin strips.

- Toss tomatoes and kale in a large bowl. Add half of the Caesar dressing and season with salt and pepper to taste.

- Divide salad between four plates and garnish with grilled chicken and additional Parm.

3.18 Mustardy potato salad with grilled Flank steak

Prep time: 30min

Serves: 4

Ingredients:

- 1 1/2 lb. of small fresh potatoes

- 1 tbsp. of grainy mustard

- 1/4 cup of freshly chopped chives and some additional for garnish

- 1 1/4 lb. flank steak, cut in 2 pieces

- 1 tbsp. of apple cider vinegar

- 1 tbsp. of kosher salt

- 3 tbsp. of extra virgin olive oil, divide in half

- 1 tbsp. of freshly ground black pepper

- 1 tsp. of ground coriander

Directions:

- Fill a big pot halfway with water and fit with a steamer basket. Bring it to a boil and cook the potatoes for 15 to 18 minutes or until they are soft. Transfer to a wide bowl after draining. Season with some salt and pepper and toss with chives, vinegar, mustard, and 1 tablespoon oil.

- In the meantime, cook the steak. In a big skillet over medium-high pressure, heat the remaining 2 tablespoons of oil. Salt, coriander, and pepper can be used to season the steak. Cook, turning once, for approximately 3-4 minutes per side, or until an instant-read thermometer put into the thickest section reads 130o for medium-rare. Transfer to a cutting board and allow to cool for 5 minutes before slicing. Serve with potatoes and chives on top.

3.19 Herbed couscous, Dijon-apricot mustard and salad with grilled sausages

Prep time: 35min

Serves: 4

- 1 to 10-oz box couscous
- 1/4 cup of apricot jam
- 1/4 cup of whole-grain Dijon mustard
- 5 tbsp. of extra virgin olive oil, divide in half
- 2 tbsp. of freshly chopped mint
- 2 tbsp. of freshly chopped basil
- 1 tbsp. of kosher salt
- 4 sausages of chicken, lamb or pork
- 1 tbsp. of freshly ground black pepper
- 6 cups of mixed greens
- Juice of a lemon

Directions:

- 1. Bring two cups of water to a boil in a saucepan. Add couscous, remove from flame, and cover. Allow staying for 5 minutes before fluffing with a fork. Spoon out couscous and allow the couscous to cool slightly in the dish.

- Mix together apricot jam and Dijon mustard in a small bowl, then put aside.

- Mix couscous with 1 tablespoon olive oil, mint, and basil. Season with salt and pepper to taste.

- Preheat a finely oiled grill pan over high heat and grill sausages for about 8 to 10 minutes, turning sides every 2 minutes, or until an internal temperature of 155° is reached.

- Whisk together remaining olive oil and lemon juice in a wide bowl; season with salt and pepper. Toss gently with mixed greens until fully covered.

- Serve sausages with salad, couscous, and Dijon-apricot mustard.

3.20 Grilled Thai coconut lime skirt steak

Prep time: 15min

Serves: 4

- ½ cup of lite coconut milk
- 2 teaspoons of lime zest
- ¼ cup of coconut sugar
- 2 tablespoons of lime juice
- 2 teaspoons of grated ginger roots
- 2 teaspoons of Thai fish sauce
- ½ teaspoon of coarse kosher salt
- 1 pound of beef skirt steak, grass fed, cut in 4 inch lengths

Directions:

- In a small bowl, whisk together lime juice, coconut sugar, coconut milk, lime zest, fish sauce, and ginger. Fill a 1-gallon resealable bag halfway with skirt steak. Put marinade evenly over the beef. Remove excess air and reseal the bag. Refrigerate the steak for 4 to 12 hours before cooking.

- Preheat the grill to the hottest temperature.

- Remove steak from marinade and discard marinade. Pat dry steaks and season with salt. Grease the grill rack and instantly put the steaks on it.

- Cook for 2 minutes and rotate 1/4 turn to make a hash mark. Cook for an additional 30 to 90 seconds on the first side. Cook for a further 2 12 to 5 minutes on the second side, for a total of 5 to 8 minutes depending on the thickness of the steaks.

- Enable steaks to rest for at least 4 minutes on the carving board before cutting lengthwise through the grain.

3.21 Spicy Peruvian green sauce with Peruvian chicken

Prep time: 20 minutes

Serves: 4

Ingredients:

1 to ½ –2 pounds of skinless and boneless chicken breast or thigh or Portobellos

Marinade:

- 4 finely minced garlic cloves
- 2 tablespoons of lime juice
- 2 tablespoons of **olive oil**
- 2 teaspoons of **honey,** agave or sugar
- 2 teaspoons of **smoked paprika**
- 1 teaspoon of **coriander**
- 1 tablespoon of **cumin**
- 1 tablespoon of fresh sub thyme or marjoram
- 1 teaspoon of **dried oregano**
- 1 ½ teaspoon of **kosher salt**
- 1 teaspoon of **soy sauce**

Peruvian green sauce (aji verde):

- ½ cup of mayo or sour cream
- 1 garlic clove
- ½ jalapeño
- ¼ teaspoon of **kosher salt**
- 1 cup of chopped cilantro with thin stems

- 1tbsp of lime squeeze (save some for the salad)

Cucumber tomato salad

- 2 cups of diced or sliced Turkish or English cucumber
- Handful of cherry tomatoes (yellow or red)
- 1 large diced perfectly ripe **avocado**
- Some cilantro leaves for garnishing
- 1 tsp. of **kosher salt**
- **Olive oil** for drizzling
- 1 tbsp. of squeeze of lime

Some optional bowl additions: Cooked **Mexican pinto beans or Cilantro lime rice**.

Directions:

- Preheat the grill to a medium-high temperature.
- If making rice, begin this on the burner.
- In a small bowl, whisk together the marinade ingredients. Finely mince the garlic and transfer it to the bowl using a garlic press. Mix the lime juice, oil, sugar, paprika, cumin, coriander, salt, oregano, and soy sauce. Stir for a few minutes. Combine it with the chicken in a bowl, be sure to coat all sides well, then put it on the Portobello. Marinate when the grill is heating up or overnight for more flavor. (Because the Portobello ingest the marinade, go easy on the marinade and reapply before grilling.)
- To create Peruvian Green Sauce, combine all ingredients in a blender and puree until smooth, scraping down the blender's sides if necessary.
- When the grill is heating, sear the chicken and Portobello on both sides (flipping with a metal spatula), either reduce the heat or move the chicken to a cooler part of the grill to finish frying. When Portobello cook, plate them and cover them with foil to keep them safe.
- To make the salad, dice the cucumbers and place them in a big small bowl. Place the avocado evenly on top. Toss in a couple of cherry tomato halves. Season with salt and pepper to taste and a drizzle of olive oil. Lime juice can be added too. Garnish with cilantro berries.
- Serve with the Cilantro Lime Rice. If making bowls, start with 3/4 cup rice in the bottom, followed by sliced chicken or Portobello on one side, avocado salad on the other, and cilantro sauce on top.

3.22 Thai Turkey burgers with crunchy Asian slaw

Prep time: 30min

Serves: 4

Ingredients:

Turkey burger:

- lb. of ground turkey
- ½ teaspoon of chopped fresh ginger
- tablespoons of finely diced shallot or red onion
- teaspoon of **granulated garlic or** 2 finely minced garlic cloves
- tablespoons of chopped mint, or Thai basil
- tablespoon of finely chopped lemongrass
- teaspoon of **sugar**
- teaspoon of lime zest
- finely chopped, seeded jalapeño, red chili sauce or 1 tablespoon **sriracha** sauce
- chopped scallion
- tablespoon of sub **soy sauce or fish sauce**
- ¼ teaspoon of **white pepper**

Crunchy Asian slaw:

- cup of grated carrots
- tablespoon of **olive oil**
- thinly sliced scallion
- 1 cup of shredded purple cabbage
- tablespoons of lime juice
- 1 teaspoon of **sugar**
- ¼ teaspoon of pepper and **salt**

Spicy aioli:

- 1/4 cup of **vegan mayo**
- 1–2 tablespoons of chili garlic sauce or **sriracha** sauce

Optional Additions: Cucumber Ribbons, toasted Buns, spicy greens like watercress, **pickled red onions**, sprouts, pickled radishes and **avocado**

Directions:

- Preheat the grill to a medium-high heat.
- In a medium mixing bowl, combine all of the burger ingredients and blend well with the fingertips. Shape them into three burgers with your wet hands. They should be 1-inch thick. Put them in the fridge on a tray.
- In a medium mixing bowl, combine all of the slaw ingredients.
- In a small bowl, mix all of the ingredients for the spicy aioli.
- Cook patties for about 4-5 minutes on each side on a well-greased, preheated grill until golden brown and cooked through.
- Grill or toast the buns.
- Sprinkle the aioli on the bottom bun, then top with the patty, cucumber ribbons, slaw, more aioli, and the top bun.

Chapter 4: Grilled Seafood Recipes

The take on grilled seafood recipes is as follows: Whether something exists in water, it belongs on fire. You will love grilling salmon (and you will really love to grill arctic char). Oysters and clams are the favorite seafood of many people to grill (and slices of bread on their side). We can enjoy grilling squid, halibut, shrimp, and whatever else you might get our hands on at the fishmonger (or order frozen.) When it comes to grilling fish, virtually everything goes from shrimp to salmon and scallops to cod to calamari and lobster. There is a compilation of a list of your favorite grilled fish recipes and seafood ideas to get you started. So, check out these best grilled seafood recipes for more grilled seafood inspiration.

4.1 Spicy grilled shrimp

Prep time: 15min

Serves: 8

Ingredients:

- 1/4 cup of extra-virgin olive oil
- minced garlic cloves
- 1/4 cup of lime juice
- tbsp. of honey
- 1 tbsp. of chili garlic sauce or Sriracha
- 2 tbsp. of low-sodium soy sauce

- 1/4 cup of freshly chopped cilantro, for garnish
- 2 lb. of peeled and deveined shrimp
- Some lime wedges, for serving

Directions:

- Whisk together lime juice, olive oil, garlic, butter, soy sauce, and chili sauce in a medium bowl. 1/4 cup marinade can be reserved for brushing on shrimp before grilling.
- Toss the shrimp with the remaining marinade in a large bowl. Preheat the grill pan or grill and skewer the shrimps.
- Grill shrimp until pink and translucent, around 3 minutes per side, brushing before and after each flip with reserved 1/4 cup marinade.
- Serve garnished with cilantro and lime wedges.

4.2 Grilled shrimp foil packets

Prep time: 25min

Serves: 4

Ingredients:

- 1 1/2 lb. peeled and deveined large shrimp
- 2 thinly sliced smoked Andouille sausages
- 2 minced cloves garlic
- 2 ears corn, cut crosswise in 4 pieces
- 2 tbsp. of extra virgin olive oil
- 1 lb. of chopped red bliss potatoes
- 1 tbsp. of Old Bay seasoning
- 1 tbsp. of freshly ground black pepper
- 2 tbsp. of kosher salt
- 1 lemon, sliced in thin wedges
- 2 tbsp. of freshly chopped parsley
- tbsp. of butter

Directions:

- Preheat grill to high or the oven to 425°. Cut four 12-inch-long sheets of aluminum.

- Divide the shrimp, sausage, garlic, corn, and potatoes among the foil sheets equally.

- Drizzle with oil, then season with Old Bay seasoning and salt and pepper to taste. Gently toss to mix. Each mixture should be garnished with lemon, parsley, and a tablespoon of butter.

- Fold crosswise the foil packets over the shrimp boil mixture to fully enclose the food.

- Seal the top and bottom edges by rolling them together.

- Place foil packets on the grill and cook for approximately 15 to 20 minutes, or until only cooked through (or transfer to an oven and bake for about 20 minutes).

4.3 Pineapple shrimp skewers

Prep time: 35min

Serves: 4

Ingredients:

- cups of cubed pineapple
- tbsp. of extra virgin olive oil
- 1 lb. of peeled and deveined shrimp
- tbsp. of sweet chili sauce
- 2 tsp. of freshly grated ginger
- 2 minced cloves of garlic
- 2 tsp. of toasted sesame oil
- ½ tbsp. of kosher salt
- 1/2 tsp. of crushed red pepper flakes
- ½ cup thinly sliced green onions, for garnish
- Toasted sesame seeds, for garnish
- Lime wedges, for serving

Directions:

- Preheat grill to a medium heat setting and soak wooden skewers in water. Skewer pineapple and shrimp alternately until both are used, then arrange on a wide baking sheet.

- Combine the olive oil, garlic, ginger, chili sauce, sesame oil, and red pepper flakes in a medium bowl and season with salt.

- Whisk together until smooth and brush all over the skewers.

- Grill skewers, turning once until the shrimp is cooked through, around 4 to 6 minutes max.

- Before eating, garnish with green onions and sesame seeds.

4.4 Perfect grilled fish

Prep time: 15min

Serves: 4

Ingredients:

- 1 tsp. of chili powder

- 1/4 tsp. of cayenne pepper

- 1 tsp. of dried oregano

- 1 tbsp. of kosher salt

- ½ inch thick fillet skin-on white fish, like cod or bass

- 1 tsp. of freshly ground black pepper

- Lime wedges, for serving

Directions:

- Preheat the grill to its hottest temperature. Combine oregano, chili powder, cayenne pepper, and salt and pepper.

- Season the fish with the spice mixture all over.

- Cook, wrapped, skin-side down, for 8 to 10 minutes, or until nearly completely opaque throughout.

- Flip and Cook for an additional 2 or 3 minutes, or until opaque throughout.

4.5 Grilled Halibut with mango salsa

Prep time: 25min

Serves: 4

Ingredients:

For the Halibut:

- (4 to 6oz) halibut steaks
- 1 tbsp. of kosher salt
- 2 tbsp. of extra virgin olive oil
- 1 tsp. freshly ground black pepper

For the mango salsa:

- 1 diced mango
- 1/2 diced red onion
- 1 finely chopped red pepper
- 1 tbsp. of freshly chopped cilantro
- 1 minced jalapeno
- 1 tbsp. of kosher salt
- Juice of a lime
- 1 tsp. of freshly ground black pepper

Directions:

- Preheat grill to medium-high flame. Brush both sides of the halibut with oil and season with salt and pepper.
- Grill halibut until it reaches an internal temperature of 145°F, around 5 minutes per side.
- **Prepare salsa:** In a medium dish, combine all ingredients and season with some salt and pepper. Serve salsa over the halibut.

4.6 Lemony grilled salmon

Prep time: 20min

Serves: 4

Ingredients:

- 4 6oz skin-on salmon fillets
- 1 tbsp. of freshly ground black pepper
- 2 sliced lemons
- 1 tbsp. of kosher salt
- 2 tbsp. of extra virgin olive oil for brushing
- 2 tbsp. of butter

Directions:

- Preheat grill to its highest setting. Season the salmon with salt and pepper after brushing with oil.
- Grill the salmon and lemon slices for 5 minutes on each side or until the salmon is cooked through and the lemons are charred.
- Serve salmon with a pat of butter just after it comes off the grill, topped with sliced lemons and serve.

4.7 Grilled tilapia

Prep time: 20min

Serves: 3

Ingredients:

- tbsp. of extra virgin olive oil, divided
- 1/4 thinly sliced small red onion
- 2 tbsp. of red wine vinegar
- 1/2 cup of grape tomatoes
- 2 tbsp. of fresh oregano leaves
- 1 tbsp. of freshly ground black pepper
- 1 tbsp. of kosher salt
- (8oz) tilapia filets

Directions:

- Preheat grill to a moderately high setting. Whisk together 2 tablespoons olive oil and 2 tablespoons red wine vinegar in a medium bowl. Season with salt and pepper and add red onion and oregano.
- Season tilapia with salt and pepper and brush with remaining olive oil.

- Preheat the grill and place fillets and grape tomatoes on it. Cook grape tomatoes for about 4 minutes, or until tender and blistered.

- Grill tilapia for around 4 minutes per side, or until the sides are opaque and the flesh instantly releases from the grill.

- Transfer fish to a serving tray. Combine grilled tomatoes and vinegar mixture in a bowl and spoon over fillets. Serve right away.

4.8 Grilled salmon with cilantro lime sauce

Prep time: 25min

Serves: 4

Ingredients:

- (6oz) of salmon fillets

- 1 tsp. of freshly ground black pepper

- 1 tbsp. of kosher salt

- tbsp. of butter

- 1/4 cup of honey

- 2 minced garlic cloves

- 2 tbsp. of chopped cilantro

- 1/2 cup of lime juice

Directions:

- Season the salmon with sea salt and freshly ground pepper. Preheat the grill and put salmon with the flesh side down on the grill. Cook for about 8 minutes, then flip and cook for another 6 minutes, just until salmon is cooked through. Allow 5 minutes for rest.

- **Meanwhile, prepare the sauce:**

- Add lime juice, butter, honey, and garlic to a medium saucepan over medium heat.

- Stir until the butter has melted and the mixture is well mixed.

- Remove from heat and stir in cilantro.

- Serve salmon with sauce.

4.9 Grilled salmon with pineapple salsa

Prep time: 25min

Serves: 4

Ingredients:

- Juice of 3 limes, divided
- 1 tsp. of honey
- 2 tbsp. of extra virgin olive oil
- 1 tbsp. of chopped fresh cilantro
- 6oz skin-on salmon fillets
- ¼ chopped red onion
- 1 1/2 cup of chopped pineapple
- 2 tbsp. of kosher salt
- 1 tbsp. of freshly ground black pepper

Directions:

- To make the sauce, whisk together the juice of two limes, olive oil, and honey in a large dish.
- Preheat grill to its highest setting. Grill salmon until cooked through, for about 5 to 6 minutes per side, brushing with honey-lime sauce.
- Meanwhile, prepare pineapple salsa by combining onion, pineapple, remaining lime juice, and cilantro in a medium bowl and seasoning with salt and pepper.
- Serve warm salmon with salsa.

4.10 Honey-lime Tilapia and corn foil pack

Prep time: 25min

Serves: 4

Ingredients:

- fillets of tilapia

- 4, thinly sliced limes

- 2 tbsp. of honey

- 2 tbsp. of honey

- 2 tbsp. of kosher salt

- 2 shucked ears corn

- 1/4 cup of extra virgin olive oil

- 1 tbsp. of freshly ground black pepper

Directions:

- Preheat grill to its highest setting. Cut four 12" long sheets of aluminum.

- Each piece of foil should be topped with a piece of tilapia. Brush the tilapia with honey and topped with corn, lime, and cilantro. Season with some salt and pepper and drizzle with olive oil.

- Grill until the tilapia is opaque and the corn is soft for around 15 minutes and serve.

4.11 Grilled shrimp tacos with sriracha slaw

Prep time: 40min

Serves: 4

Ingredients:

- 1/4 cup of extra virgin olive oil

- Juice of 3 limes, divided

- tbsp. of freshly chopped cilantro

- 2 tbsp. of kosher salt

- 1 lb. peeled and deveined large shrimp

- 1 tbsp. of freshly ground black pepper

- 1/4 head shredded red cabbage

- 1 tbsp. of sriracha

- 1/4 cup of mayonnaise

- medium tortillas

Directions:

- Combine cilantro, olive oil, and 1/3 of the lime juice in a small bowl. Season with sea salt and freshly ground pepper.

- Pour mixture over shrimp in a baking dish. Toss until evenly covered and set aside for 20 minutes to marinate.

- Meanwhile, prepare the slaw: Toss cabbage in a big bowl of remaining lime juice, mayo and Sriracha. Season with some salt and pepper.

- Preheat grill to its highest setting. Grill shrimp on skewers until charred, around 3 minutes each side.

- Grill tortillas for 1 minute per side until charred.

- To serve, wrap shrimp in the tortillas and top with slaw.

4.12 Foil pack grilled salmon with lemony asparagus

Prep time: 20min

Serves: 4

Ingredients:

- 20 trimmed asparagus spears
- tbsp. of butter, divided
- 2 sliced lemons
- 6oz skin-on salmon fillets
- 1 tbsp. of freshly ground black pepper
- 2 tbsp. of kosher salt
- Torn fresh dill for garnish

Directions:

- On a flat surface, place two pieces of foil. Arrange five asparagus spears on foil and top with a salmon fillet, add 1 tablespoon of butter, and two lemon slices. Wrap loosely and repeat with the remaining ingredients till you have four packages in all.

- Preheat grill to full heat. Grill the foil packets for around 10 minutes, or until the salmon is cooked through and the asparagus is soft.

- Serve garnished with dill.

4.13 Mediterranean salmon skewer

Prep time: 20min

Serves: 4

Ingredients:

- sliced lemons
- 2 tbsp. of extra virgin olive oil, for brushing
- 1 lb. of salmon fillets, use wild, cut into 2 inch pieces
- 1 tsp. of ground black pepper
- 1 tbsp. of kosher salt
- Torn fresh dill, for garnish

Directions:

- Preheat grill to its highest setting. Lemon slices and salmon are skewered and then brushed with some olive oil and season with some salt and ground black pepper.
- Grill the skewers till salmon is cooked inside, for about 6-8 minutes per side.
- Serve garnished with dill.

4.14 Party shrimp boil

Prep time: 45min

Serves: 8

Ingredients:

- 1 1/2 lb. peeled and deveined large shrimp,
- 2 smoked thinly sliced Andouille sausages
- 2 minced cloves of garlic
- 2 ears corn, cut crosswise into 4 pieces
- 2 tbsp. of extra virgin olive oil
- 1 lb. chopped red bliss potatoes
- tsp. of Old Bay seasoning, divided
- tbsp. of melted butter
- 1 lemon, sliced in thin wedges

- 1 tbsp. of freshly ground black pepper

- 2 tbsp. of kosher salt

- 2 tbsp. of fresh parsley leaves, chopped and divided

Directions:

- Preheat grill to a medium-high temperature.

- In a medium saucepan, mix potatoes, water, and salt. Bring water to a boil and then reduce to low heat and cook until potatoes are soft.

- Meanwhile, add shrimp, garlic, olive oil, 2 tsp. Old Bay, and 1 tbsp. Parsley in a medium dish.

- Toss the shrimp until coated uniformly. Allow 15 minutes for marinating.

- Combine maize, boiled potatoes, 1 tsp. Old Bay, melted butter, and 1 tbsp. Parsley in a separate medium dish.

- On metal skewers, thread shrimp, potatoes, lemon, sausage, and corn (or wooden skewers that must have been soaked for approximately 20 minutes).

- Grill the skewers until shrimp are opaque, and lemon is charred, for about 4-5 minutes overall, flipping halfway through.

4.15 Grilled shrimp tostadas with red cabbage slaw and guacamole

Prep time: 30min

Serves: 4

Ingredients:

- 8 (6 inch) corn tortillas

- ripe diced avocados

- 2 tbsp. of canola oil or cooking spray

- 2 tsp. of cumin

- 1 minced small shallot

- tbsp. of freshly chopped cilantro

- 7 tbsp. of lime juice, divided

- 2 tbsp. of kosher salt

- 1/4 cup of extra virgin olive oil, divided

- 1/2 tsp. of cayenne
- 24 medium peeled and deveined shrimp
- 1/4 cup of finely shredded red cabbage
- 3/4 cup of finely shredded carrots (1 large carrot)
- 1 tbsp. of freshly ground black pepper
- Some lime wedges, for serving
- Some cilantro leaves, for serving

Directions:

- Preheat oven to 400 degrees Fahrenheit.
- Arrange four tortillas on each of two baking sheets sprayed with canola oil spray. Spray tortillas with additional oil and bake for about 8 minutes, or until golden brown and crisp.
- Mash avocados, 3 teaspoons lime juice, shallot and cilantro in a medium bowl. Season with salt.
- Whisk together Cumin, 2 teaspoons lime juice, cayenne and 2 tablespoons olive oil in a large bowl. Season shrimp generously with some salt and pepper and toss gently to cover.
- Grill shrimp for 3 minutes per side over a medium-high flame or turn bright pink and cooked through.
- Toss cabbage and carrot in a wide bowl with the remaining 2 tablespoons of lime juice and 2 tablespoons of olive oil. Season with sea salt and freshly ground pepper.
- Arrange tostadas in a single layer on a flat work surface and top with guacamole. Serve with lime and garnish with slaw, shrimp, and cilantro leaves.

4.16 Tomato gazpacho with grilled shrimp and avocado

Prep time: 25 min

Serves: 4

Ingredients:

- 1 1/2 lb. cored and roughly chopped red heirloom tomatoes
- 1/4 finely chopped red onion

- 1 peeled, seeded, and roughly chopped English cucumber
- 1/3 cup of finely chopped fresh cilantro (and some more leaves for garnish)
- 3/4 tsp. of crushed red pepper flakes
- 2 minced cloves of garlic (divided)
- 5 tbsp. of extra virgin olive oil, divided (and some more for serving)
- 2 tbsp. of kosher salt
- tbsp. of sherry vinegar
- 12 (10 to 15 ct.) shrimp, cleaned with the tails left on
- 1 tbsp. of freshly ground black pepper
- 1 tbsp. of lemon juice
- 1 1/2 tsp. of ground cumin
- 1/2 diced avocado

Directions:

- Combine tomatoes, red onion, cucumber, cilantro, 1 garlic clove, sherry vinegar, 1/4 teaspoon red pepper flakes, and 4 tablespoons olive oil in a wide bowl; season with some salt and pepper.

- Blend half of the tomato mixture until creamy in a blender. Pour leftover tomato mixture into a clean bowl and make the puree, and add it to gazpacho. Season with extra salt and pepper to taste, then chill until ready to eat.

- Combine shrimp, lemon juice, cumin, remaining 1 garlic clove, 1 tablespoon of olive oil in a large bowl, and then gently mix and season with some salt and pepper.

- Grill shrimp for about 1 minute on either side and another minute in the center (3 minutes maximum) or until bright pink and only cooked through.

- Distribute gazpacho evenly among four bowls and top with diced avocado, cilantro leaves, grilled shrimp, and a drizzle of olive oil. Serve right away.

4.17 Blackened Salmon with tomato, avocado and corn salad

Prep time: 25 min

Serves: 4

Ingredients:

- (5oz) pieces of wild salmon

- 1 1/2 tsp. of brown sugar
- 1 1/2 tsp. of coriander
- 1 1/2 tsp. of chili powder
- 6 tbsp. of extra virgin olive oil, divided
- 2 tbsp. of kosher salt
- 1/2 thinly sliced shallot
- ears of corn, kernels removed
- tbsp. of red wine vinegar
- 1/2 pt. of red grape tomatoes, halved
- 1 1/2 diced avocados
- 1/2 pt. of yellow table tomatoes, halved
- 1 tbsp. of freshly ground black pepper
- 1/4 cup of finely chopped fresh cilantro

Directions:

- Preheat oven to 400 degrees Fahrenheit. On a pan, arrange salmon skin-side down.
- Combine brown sugar, coriander, and chili powder in a small bowl and season with salt. Incorporate mixture into salmon.
- Allow red wine vinegar and shallots to sit in a small bowl. Combine corn, avocados, tomatoes, and cilantro in a big bowl.
- In a big nonstick ovenproof skillet, heat 3 tablespoons of olive oil over medium-high heat until nearly smoking. 2 minutes skin-side up, sear salmon fillets. Switch skillet to oven and cook for an additional 3 minutes, or until salmon is only cooked through.
- Combine red wine vinegar, shallots, and remaining 3 tablespoons of olive oil in corn mixture. Season with sea salt and freshly ground pepper and serve

4.18 Easy grilled Mahi with corn and avocado salsa

Prep time: 25 min

Serves: 4

Ingredients:

- thawed Mahi Mahi fillets

- 2 teaspoons of ground cumin
- 2 teaspoons of chili powder
- 2 tablespoons of olive oil
- 1/4 teaspoon of pepper
- 1/2 teaspoon of salt

For corn salsa:

- 2 fresh ears of corn shucked and removed from the cob
- 1 firm cubed ripe avocado
- 1 seeded and chopped small poblano pepper
- 1/3 cup of chopped purple onion
- 1/2 cup chopped red pepper
- tablespoons of olive oil
- 1 tablespoon of vinegar
- 1 tablespoon of sugar
- 1/4 teaspoon of pepper
- 1/2 teaspoon of salt

Directions:

For the Salsa:

Combine all the ingredients in a large bowl. Chill them while fish is grilling.

For Mahi:

- Preheat an indoor or outdoor grill to a medium-high temperature.
- Combine cumin, olive oil, chili powder, salt, and pepper in a shallow bowl.
- Spread it to uncooked Mahi fillets with a brush.
- Grill for about 4 minutes on either side (depending on the fillet's thickness) or until the fish reaches an internal temperature of 145 degrees and quickly flakes.
- Serve alongside Salsa!

4.19 Grilled salmon with mango salsa

Prep time: 25 min

Serves: 4

Ingredients:

- (6oz) salmon fillets
- 1 tsp. of chili powder
- 1 tsp. of garlic powder
- 1 tsp. of pepper
- 1 tbsp. of salt
- Juice of a lime

Mango salsa:

- 2 to 3 diced mangoes
- 1 seeded and finely chopped small jalapeno
- ½ diced red pepper
- ¼ cup roughly chopped packed cilantro leaves

Directions:

- Combine mangos, onions, red peppers, jalapenos, and cilantro in a medium bowl. Remove from heat and set aside until ready to use.
- Combine chili powder, garlic powder, salt, and pepper in a small bowl (you can use around 1/2 teaspoon of each). Salmon fillets should be rubbed with the mixture. Grill for 6-8 minutes on either side over medium heat.
- Serve grilled salmon with fresh lime juice and mango salsa on top.

4.20 Grilled fish taco burrito bowls

Prep time: 30 min

Serves: 4

Ingredients:

Tortilla bowls:

- (8 inch) round flour tortillas
- 1 tbsp. of salt
- 1 tbsp. of nonstick spray
- 1 tsp. of pepper

Grilled Fish:

- fish filets with skin removed
- 2 cloves of garlic
- 1 shallot
- 1 jalapeno stemmed and seeded
- 1 tablespoon of hot sauce
- 2 tablespoons of olive oil
- 1 tablespoon of chipotle chili powder
- 1 tbsp. of salt
- 1 teaspoon of ground cumin
- 1 tbsp. of black pepper

Fruit salsa:

- 1 large peeled, pitted and diced mango
- 1 large pitted and diced small peach
- 1 cup of diced strawberries
- 1 tsp. of salt
- 1 seeded, stemmed and minced jalapeno pepper
- 1/4 cup of chopped cilantro
- 1/4 cup of diced red onion
- 1 teaspoon of lime juice
- 1 tsp. of pepper

Fish taco burrito bowls:

- to 5 tortilla bowls
- grilled fish filets cut into pieces
- 1 cup of cilantro lime rice
- 2 avocados mashed with some salt and black pepper
- cups of chopped romaine lettuce
- 1 cup of sour cream
- Some chopped cilantro

Directions:

Tortilla bowls:

- Preheat oven to 400 degrees Fahrenheit. Prepare 2-4 oven-safe bowls by inverting them on a baking sheet.

- If you have just two oven-safe bowls, this would have to be done in batches. Spray one side of each tortilla with nonstick spray.

- Season with salt and freshly ground black pepper and arrange them spray-side down in the upside-down bowls. Shape a slight ring around the bowl by pressing. They will not adhere fully, but they will begin to take form.

- Bake the tortillas for 12-15 minutes, or until they are brown and crispy.

- Remove from heat and carefully remove the tortillas from the bowls. Set them aside, and repeat if necessary.

Grilled fish:

- In the bowl of the food processor, combine the shallot, jalapeno and garlic. Pulse until the mixture is pureed. Add the mixture to a large and shallow bowl.

- Whisk in the olive oil, chipotle chili powder, hot sauce, cumin, and a generous amount of salt and black pepper.

- Add the fish to the dish and flip it to coat. Let it marinate while you prepare the rest of the ingredients.

- Once marinated, preheat the grill over medium high heat.

- Add the fish to the grill and cook for about 3-4 minutes on each side, or until it is cooked through. Remove it from heat and set aside.

Fruit salsa:

- In a medium bowl, mix the mango, red onion, strawberries, peach, cilantro, lime juice, and a dash of salt and black pepper.

- Toss it to combine and set aside.

4.21 Grilled Branzino with preserved lemon Gremolata

Prep Time: 15 minutes

Serves: 2

Ingredients

- 1 tablespoon of **olive oil**

- 1 teaspoon of **sea salt**

- 1 whole branzino descaled, gutted and cleaned (roughly 1.25- 2lbs)

- 1/2 teaspoon of pepper
- A handful of fresh herbs. thyme, rosemary, sage or parsley
- 1 lemon

Preserved lemon gremolata:

- 1/4 cup of preserved and chopped lemons
- 2 finely chopped garlic cloves
- 1 bunch of finely chopped flat-leaf parsley, with tender stems, about 1 cup
- 1/2 cup of olive oil
- 2 tbsp. of cracked pepper
- 2 tbsp. of chili flakes (optional)

Directions:

- While you are buying a whole fish, ensure that it has been gutted and descaled.
- Rinse it thoroughly from inside and out, then pat it dry completely
- Add a good amount of oil in it.
- Season both inside and outside of the fish with salt and pepper.
- Peel some lemons and put them within the fish's cavity. Put fresh herbs like rosemary, thyme, sage, or parsley.
- Cut 2-3 slits on each side of the fish's thicker end with a sharp knife. Since the tail end burns quicker than the head end, the grill will cook more equally.
- Spray the grates and fire the grill to a medium-high heat, about 400F. Reduce the heat to one side if possible.
- Put the fish on a greased and hot grill, with the tail end on the cooler side of the grill. Grill a 1 1/2-2 pound fish for around 5 minutes, without moving it, or until grill marks appears.
- Carefully flip it with tongs and a thin metal spatula. Cover and grill for another 4-5 minutes, or until grill marks appears on the fish.
- Make the flavorful sauce while the fish is grilling. To make the preserved lemon gremolata, add all of the Ingredients to a large bowl and stir well.
- Place the fish on a platter and spoon the flavorful Gremolata on top just before serving. Also, eat the delicious crispy skin!
- Serve it with a leafy green salad and Everyday Quinoa.

4.22 Grilled salmon Tzatziki bowl

Prep Time: 15 minutes

Serves: 4

Ingredients

- 2 tbsp. of olive oil for brushing
- One lemon- sliced in half
- 8 to 10 ounces salmon
- 1 tbsp. of pepper
- 2 tbsp. of salt

Optional bowl additions:

- Add any fresh vegetables you prefer like tomatoes, radishes, cucumber or sprouts
- Fresh herbs, olive oil, and lemon for garnish.
- Cooked rice or Quinoa, arugula or any other greens, grilled veggies like zucchini, tomatoes, eggplant, or peppers.

Directions:

- Preheat the grill to a medium-high temperature.
- Cook one cup rice or quinoa on the stove. (Quinoa needs just 15 to 20 minutes to prepare.)
- Season the salmon with salt and pepper after brushing it with olive oil and set aside.
- Tzatziki Sauce can be made or purchased.
- Place the salmon and any other vegetables you want to grill on the grill (season with some salt and pepper and brush with olive oil).
- Grill the salmon for about 3-4 minutes on both sides, depending on the cut's thickness. Now grill the lemon, open side down, until it has a nice grill mark. (Just before serving, squeeze the grilled lemon over the salmon.)
- Assemble the two bowls until the vegetables and salmon are cooked.
- Divide the quinoa between the two bowls. Put a couple of greens on top. Add any fresh vegetables you like, drizzle with some olive oil, and season with salt and pepper.
- Over the top, arrange the salmon and the grilled vegetables. Squeeze the grilled lemon over the bowl as a final touch.

- Top the salmon with a few spoonful of tzatziki sauce and serve. Fresh dill or other herbs can be sprinkled on top as well.

Chapter 5: Grilled snacks and desserts

Not everyone is capable of being in control of the main course. Here are some recipes for appetizers, snacks, hors d'oeuvres, and side dishes that will get the relatives swarming around the little Smoky Joe rather than taking their normal seats next to Uncle Jesse's burger station. As summer is officially over for the year, it ensures there is no need to prepare in the kitchens. Since it's so hot in there, you must be thinking about going outside and preheating the grill. And you don't want to confine yourself to the traditional. Although burgers are delicious and you must be happy to serve them, they cannot be the only item on the menu. To ensure that you serve your guests only the finest grilled snacks and appetizers, this book includes a few recipes for delicious grilled snacks and desserts.

5.1 Grilled figs stuffed with goat cheese

Prep time: 30 min

Serves: 4

Ingredients:

- 20 ripe figs
- 2 tablespoons of olive oil
- 4oz of soft goat cheese
- 1 tablespoon of roughly chopped fresh rosemary
- 2 tablespoons of balsamic vinegar

Directions:

- Remove the stem from each fig and then cut two slits in an X fashion from the top to 3/4 of the way down, forming a pocket in the center of the fig.

- Stuff approximately 1 teaspoon goat cheese into each fig.

- When all of the charcoal is lit and covered in grey ash, pour out and uniformly distribute the coals over the whole surface of the coal grate.

- Place the cooking grate on the grill and cover it for 5 minutes to preheat. Clean and lubricate the grill grate.

- Brush figs lightly with olive oil and put on the grill. Cover and cook them over medium heat for around 5 to 8 minutes, or until figs are softened and starting to brown slightly.

- Transfer figs to a serving tray and sprinkle some rosemary and drizzle with balsamic vinegar. Serve right away.

5.2 Bacon-wrapped crimini mushrooms

Prep time: 3o min

Serves: 4

Ingredients:

- 1 lb. of bacon, cut in half

- 2 tbsp. of olive oil

- 1 lb. of crimini mushrooms, stems removed and scrubbed

- 1 tbsp. of freshly ground black pepper

- 1 tbsp. of kosher salt

- Bamboo skewers, must be soaked in water for 30 minutes before use

Directions:

- In a large bowl, combine the mushrooms. Toss with 3-4 tablespoons olive oil until all mushrooms are well covered. Season to taste with salt and pepper.

- Wrap half a slice of bacon around each mushroom and thread into skewers, allowing at least 1/2 inch of space for each mushroom.

- One complete chimney of charcoal should be lit. Once all of the charcoal is lit and coated in grey ash, pour it out and scatter it uniformly over the charcoal grate.

- The cooking grate should be cleaned and oiled. Grill the mushroom skewers until the bacon is fried and crisp on all sides, realigning the skewers as required to avoid flare-ups.

- Serve immediately or at room temperature.

5.3 Planked goat cheese stuffed Peppadews

Prep time: 30 to 40 min

Serves: 6 to 8

Ingredients:

- ounces of spreadable goat cheese

- 1 tablespoon of finely chopped parsley

- 1 (14-ounce) jar of drained Peppadews

- 2 tablespoons of finely chopped chives and divided

- 1 wood plank, must be soaked in water for maximum 1 hour before use

- 1 tablespoon of extra virgin olive oil

- A small chunk of light smoking wood, such as cherry or apple

Directions:

- Combine goat cheese, parsley and 1 1/2 teaspoon chives in a small bowl.

- Fill a piping bag* fitted with a circular tip with the mixture.

- Fill Peppadews with herbed goat cheese. Drizzle stuffed Peppadews with extra-virgin olive oil and arrange on a wood plank.

- If you do not have a piping bag, a Ziploc bag with a slight cut in the corner will work.

- Once all of the charcoal is ignited and coated in grey ash, pour out and position the coals on one side of the charcoal grate, directly on top of the wood chunk.

- Place the cooking grate on the grill and cover it for 5 minutes to preheat. Place planked Peppadews on the cool side of the grill, cover, and cook for 15-25 minutes, or until the Peppadews begin to brown in spots.

- Serve immediately after removing from grill and sprinkling with remaining 1/2 tbsp. of chives.

5.4 Yaki Onigiri

Prep time: 20 min

Serves: 4

Ingredients:

- 1/4 cup of soy sauce for glazing

- 2 cups of white rice or 3 cups of cooked short-grain white rice, and 1 cup of brown rice

Directions:

- Wet your hands and scoop rice balls between your cupped palms, roughly 2/3 cup rice per ball. Compress and squeeze the rice balls into a triangular formation.

- Brush the soy sauce over the onigiri and put aside before ready to grill. Onigiri can be prepared ahead of time and stored wrapped at room temperature for many hours.

- Cook yaki onigiri on the grill's outer edges, taking care not to smoke the rice. Carefully place the balls on the grate and allow the bottom sides to harden and brown for approximately 10 minutes before flipping them.

- With a pair of tongs, gently flip the onigiri to avoid breaking the compacted onigiri. Brown for about ten minutes, on the other hand.

- Serve directly, with additional soy sauce for dipping.

5.5 Grilled Italian-style meatballs with Parmesan and Pecorino

Prep time: 30 min

Serves: 4 to 6

Ingredients:

- 1 pound of ground chuck

- 3/4 cup of fresh bread crumbs

- 1/2 pound of ground pork

- 2 lightly beaten large eggs

- 1/3 cup of grated Pecorino Romano

- 1/3 cup of grated Parmesan

- 2 minced cloves of garlic

- 1/4 teaspoon of red pepper flakes
- 2 tablespoons of finely chopped fresh parsley
- 1 tbsp. of freshly ground black pepper
- 1 tbsp. of kosher salt
- 2 tbsp. of Olive oil

Directions:

- Combine chuck, bacon, eggs, bread crumbs, and parmesan, garlic, Pecorino, parsley, and red pepper flakes in a big mixing bowl until well mixed. Roll meat mixture into 1 1/2-inch-diameter cube. Season meatballs liberally with some salt and pepper on all sides.
- When all of the charcoal is lit and coated in grey ash, spill out and uniformly distribute the coals over the whole surface of the coal grate.
- Place the cooking grate on the grill and cover it for 5 minutes to preheat. Clean and lubricate the grill grate.
- Brush meatballs with some olive oil and put on the grill. Cook for around 8 minutes overall, 2 minutes per side, or until well browned and cooked through.
- Transfer meatballs to a serving platter and set aside for 5 minutes to rest. Serve with marinara sauce on the side.

5.6 Armadillo Eggs (Sausage-Wrapped, Cheese-Stuffed, Grilled Jalapeños)

Prep time: 1 hour and 15 min

Serves: 4

Ingredients:

- ounces of cream cheese
- 1 tablespoon of finely chopped cilantro
- 1/2 cup of shredded sharp cheddar cheese
- large jalapeños, seeded and halved
- 1 tablespoon of your favorite barbecue rub
- 2 pounds of loose breakfast sausage
- 1 small piece of a light smoking wood, such as cherry or apple

Directions:

- Combine cheddar cheese, cream cheese, and cilantro in a medium bowl.

- Fill each jalapeno half halfway with a spoonful of the cream cheese mixture. Every jalapeno should be cut into two equal bits.

- Break off a 1 1/2-inch-diameter ball of sausage. Flatten sausage into a 1/4-inch wide disc and center with stuffed jalapeno.

- Wrap sausage full around jalapeno, pinching sausage closed to it. Roll the sausage gently in your hands to form a smooth egg shape. Repeat for the rest of the sausage and jalapenos.

- Once all of the charcoal is lit and coated in grey ash, spill it out and place it on one side of the charcoal grate. Place the cooking grate on the grill and cover it for 5 minutes to preheat.

- Clean and lubricate the grill grate. Directly on top of the coals, position smoking wood. Sprinkle barbecue rub evenly over armadillo eggs and cover with a top air vent located over the cool side of the grill.

- Cook for about 30 minutes, tossing eggs halfway through until sausage is cooked through and evenly browned. Some eggs that are not fully browned can be seared easily on the grill's hot side, around 1 minute per side.

- Transfer to a serving platter and set aside for 5 to 10 minutes before serving.

5.7 Grilled Sriracha hot wings

Prep time: 1 hour

Serves: 4

Ingredients:

- Pounds of chicken wings, cut into flats and drumettes

- 1 teaspoon of kosher salt

- 1 tablespoon of baking powder

For the sauce:

- tablespoons of butter

- 2 tablespoons of honey

- 1/2 cup of sriracha

- 1 1/2 tablespoons of soy sauce

- 1 tablespoon of freshly squeezed lime juice

- 1 tablespoon of finely chopped cilantro

- 1 teaspoon of rice vinegar

Directions:

- With paper towels, pat chicken wings dry. Toss wings in a wide bowl of salt and baking powder, coating uniformly.
- Arrange wings on a wire rack set over a baking sheet in a single layer. Refrigerate for at least 8 hours, uncovered.
- In a small saucepan over low heat, melt the butter. Sriracha, soy sauce, honey, cilantro, lime juice, and vinegar can be whisked in until mixed. Take the pan off the heat and put it aside.
- Once all of the charcoal is lit and coated in grey ash, spill it out and place it on one side of the charcoal grate. Place the cooking grate on the grill and cover it for 5 minutes to preheat. Clean and lubricate the grill grate.
- Cook wings skin side up over the grills' cool side, covered, for 30 to 40 minutes, or until the skins are crisp and browned. Brush sauce all over the wings, cover, and continue cooking for 5 to 10 minutes longer, or before the sauce bakes in.
- Transfer wings to a wide bowl using a large spoon. Toss wings in remaining sauce to coat uniformly. Serve immediately after transferring wings to a platter.

5.8 Pig candy recipe

Prep time: 35 min

Serves: 4

Ingredients:

- 1/2 cup of dark brown sugar
- 1 lb. of thick cut bacon
- 1/8 teaspoon of cayenne pepper
- 1/4 cup of maple syrup

Directions:

- Combine cayenne pepper and brown sugar in a small bowl.
- Arrange bacon strips in a single layer on a wire rack within a foil-lined baking sheet. Drizzle 2/3 of the brown sugar mixture on the top of bacon strips.
- Once all of the charcoal is lit and coated in grey ash, spill it out and place it on one side of the charcoal grate.

- Place the cooking grate on the grill and cover it for 5 minutes to preheat. Place the whole baking sheet with bacon on the grill rack, cover, cook for around 15 minutes, or until the sugar begins to caramelize and the bacon begins to crisp around the edges.

- Brush maple syrup on one side of the bacon slices, then flip and brush the other side with syrup. Sprinkle with leftover brown sugar mixture, cover them, and steam for an additional 10 to 15 minutes, or until bacon is thoroughly crisped.

- Remove from grill, allow to cool slightly before serving.

5.9 Grilled smashed potatoes

Prep time: 1 hour

Serves: 4

Ingredients:

- 16 small potatoes, mix variety of white, red, or purple skinned
- 1 tbsp. of freshly ground black pepper
- 2 tablespoons of roughly chopped fresh rosemary leaves and divided
- 2 tablespoons of olive oil
- 1 tbsp. of kosher salt

Directions:

- Scrub the potatoes and placed them in a medium saucepan. Pour in enough cool water to cover the potatoes. Bring water to a boil over medium-high heat, add 1 tablespoon kosher salt and reduce to low heat.

- Cook potatoes until a paring knife easily slides into the middle for around 20 minutes. Strain potatoes and allow them to cool until they are not so hot to touch.

- Arrange potatoes in a single layer on a baking sheet. Gently squeeze each potato between your palms before split open but not broken.

- Brush the potatoes with olive oil and season with salt, pepper, and half of the rosemary. Flip them over and brush oil, and season on the second side.

- When all of the charcoal is lit and coated in grey ash, spill out and uniformly distribute the coals over the whole surface of the coal grate. Place the cooking grate on the grill and cover it for 5 minutes to preheat.

- Clean and grease the grill grate. Place potatoes on grill and cook for around 5 minutes per side, or until lightly browned and crisped.

- Transfer potatoes to a serving platter and sprinkle some remaining rosemary to taste.

5.10 Scallops and shrimp with lemony soy

Prep time: 30 min

Serves: 4

Ingredients:

- 1 ½ cups of low- sodium soy sauce
- 1 cup of sake
- 1 cup of mirin
- 2 very thinly sliced lemons
- 1 pound of shelled and deveined medium shrimp
- 2 very thinly sliced jalapenos
- 2 tbsp. of vegetable oil for grilling
- 1 pound of large sea scallops

Directions:

- Mix the soy sauce, sake, mirin, lemon slices, and jalapenos in a ceramic baking dish or glass.
- Thread 8 pairs of bamboo skewers with shrimp and add to the marinade, rotating to coat. Carry out the same procedure for the scallops. Refrigerate for 30 minutes, rotating halfway through, and then drain.
- Prepare a grill by lighting it and oiling the grates. Brush the scallops and shrimp with oil and cook, rotating once or twice, for around 4 minutes, or until finely charred. Serve immediately with grilled scallions, eggplant, and a drizzle of olive oil.

5.11 Grilled vegetable gazpacho

Prep time: 45 min

Serves: 10

Ingredients:

- 2 cored and quartered large red bell peppers
- 2 unpeeled garlic cloves

- 1 tbsp. of freshly ground black pepper
- 2 cored and quartered large yellow bell peppers
- 2 medium size sliced zucchini
- 2 husked ear of corns
- A large white onion, must be cut in ½ inch slabs
- 1 tbsp. of kosher salt
- ½ tsp. of crushed red pepper
- 1 ½ tsp. of ground cumin
- ½ cup of fresh orange juice
- 2 tbsp. of red wine vinegar
- ¼ cup of chopped cilantro
- 1 thinly sliced English cucumber
- 2 cups of tomato juice
- 2 tbsp. of fresh lemon juice

Directions:

- Preheat the grill. Thread the garlic cloves into a skewer. Season the garlic, zucchini, bell peppers, onion, and corn with salt and pepper. Grill the vegetables, frequently turning, over medium-high heat until mildly charred and crisp-tender, around 10 minutes.

- Transfer the peppers to a bowl and cover with plastic wrap; set aside for 10 minutes to steam. Meanwhile, peel the garlic cloves and transfer them to a wide bowl after removing them from the skewers.

- Cut the charred corn kernels in the bowl with a big serrated knife. Peel the peppers and mix them with zucchini, cumin, onion, crushed red pepper, orange juice, lemon juice, tomato juice, and vinegar in a large mixing cup.

- Puree the vegetable mixture in batches in a food processor or blender or. Season the gazpacho with salt and pepper in a clean dish. Refrigerate covered and chill for almost 2 hours.

- Stir the cilantro in the gazpacho just before serving. Serve the soup in bowls garnished with cucumber.

Grilled Desserts

You can grill the main course and sides, but do you know you can grill desserts as well? It's easy enough to roast chicken and serve lemonade in red Solo cups... so what about dessert? It may be a little more intimidating. There is a limit on how many occasions you can serve sliced fruit until your family begins to give you the "watermelon again?" eye roll.   If grilling and eating outside are two of the most enjoyable aspects of summer, why return indoors for dessert? This book has compiled a list of many decadent grilled desserts that you can make together in minutes.

5.12 Grilled pineapple sundaes

Prep time: 10 min

Serves: 4

Ingredients:

- slices of pineapple

- scoops of vanilla ice cream

- 2 tbsp. of toasted sweetened shredded coconut

- Some Dulce de leche, for drizzling

Directions:

- Preheat grill to its highest setting. Grill pineapple for 1 minute per side until charred.

- Every pineapple slice should be drizzled with caramel or Dulce de leche and topped with vanilla ice cream. Serve immediately garnished with shredded coconut.

5.13 Foil pack S'mores roll-up

Prep time: 10 min

Serves: 1

Ingredients:

- A flour tortilla

- 1 handful of chocolate chips

- 1 handful of mini marshmallows

- 2 graham crackers

Directions:

- Tear a 12-inch by 12-inch square of foil.

- Put a tortilla on foil and line one side with chocolate chips, marshmallows, and smashed graham crackers. Cover the tortilla tightly by holding as many of the ingredients inside as possible and then wrapping tightly in foil.

- When ready to cook, put the wrapped tortilla on a hot grill or over an open flame and cook for approximately 5 minutes.

- Take the skewers off from the grill and unwrap from one hand and serve

5.14 Grilled donut ice cream sandwich

Prep time: 15 min

Serves: 4

Ingredients:

- glazed donuts, must be cut in half

- Some chocolate syrup, for drizzling

- 8 scoops of vanilla ice cream

- maraschino cherries

- 1 ½ cups of whipped cream

Directions:

- Preheat the grill pan or grill to the highest setting. Grill donut pieces, glazed side down, for around 1 minute or until charred. Allow it to cool.

- Put 2 scoops of vanilla ice cream in each donut sandwich and press.

- Drizzle each with chocolate syrup, whipped cream, and, of course, a cherry.

5.15 Grilled summer fruit skewers

Prep time: 15 min

Serves: 8

Ingredients:

- sliced peaches

- A pineapple, cut in large cubes

- 1 pt. of sliced strawberries
- 8 skewers, must be soaked in water for about 20 minutes
- 2 tbsp. of kosher salt
- 2 tbsp. of extra virgin olive oil, for drizzling
- Some honey, for drizzling

Directions:

- Preheat grill to a medium-high temperature. Skewer the strawberries, peaches, and mango. Season with salt and drizzle with olive oil.
- Grill, rotating periodically, for 10 to 12 minutes, or until fruit is tender and mildly charred.
- Drizzle honey on top.

5.16 Foil pack chocolate marshmallow banana

Prep time: 10 min

Serves: 10

Ingredients:

- 1 banana
- 1 handful of mini marshmallows
- 1 handful of chocolate chips

Directions:

- Tear a 12-inch by 12-inch square of foil.
- On foil, position the peeled banana and cut it lengthwise around 3/4 of the way across. Divide it into parts and stuff with chocolate chips and marshmallows. Cover bananas tightly in foil.
- When ready to cook, put banana wrapped in foil on a hot grill or over an open flame for approximately 5 minutes.
- Take the skewers off the grill, unwrap them, and enjoy!

5.17 Grilled banana splits

Prep time: 9 min

Serves: 4

Ingredients:

- bananas
- 1 pt. of vanilla ice cream or your favorite ice cream flavor
- tbsp. of butter
- 1 Heath candy bar or Butterfinger
- 1/2 cup of chocolate syrup
- 1 cup of whipped cream

Directions:

- Preheat grill to high heat. Brush the bananas' cut sides with melted butter and arrange them cut side down on the heated grill grate. Cook over medium-high heat for around 2 minutes, or until bananas are lightly golden and grill marks appear. Turn skin side down and continue grilling for an additional 2 minutes or until tender.
- To assemble the sundaes:
- Peel the bananas and place two halves in each of the four bowls.
- Scoop a small amount of ice cream in each bowl.
- Drizzle chocolate syrup over the top and garnish with minced sugar. If you want, garnish with whipped cream.

5.18 Grilled apricots with vanilla ice cream and brioche

Prep time: 15 min

Serves: 4

Ingredients:

- 8 ripe apricots
- 2 tbsp. of sugar
- 2 tbsp. of unsalted butter
- slice of brioche, about 1 inch thick
- 2 cups of vanilla ice cream
- 2 tbsp. of warm honey

Directions:

- Preheat a gas grill to medium-high heat or prepare a barbecue grill for direct grilling over medium-high heat. Drizzle melted butter over apricot halves and sprinkle with honey.

- Grill 1 minute per side of the brioche slices; and 2 or 3 minutes per side for apricots. Transfer brioche slices evenly among four individual serving plates. Top with apricot pieces, four to each slice. Drizzle honey on top and a swirl of vanilla ice cream and serve.

5.19 Caramelized pineapple sundaes with coconut

Prep time: 30 min

Serves: 10

Ingredients:

- A pineapple

- 2 tsp. of vegetable oil

- 2 1/2 cups of fat-free vanilla frozen yogurt

- 1/2 cup of sweetened shredded coconut

- Some mint sprigs

Directions:

- Fire up the grill. Brush some Vegetable oil on the pineapple rings. Grill, occasionally rotating, over medium-high heat until the pineapple is finely charred and softened around 8 minutes. Cut the rings into bite-size pieces after transferring them to a work surface.

- Toast the coconut in a medium skillet over moderate heat until golden, around 2 minutes. Transfer to a cooling plate.

- Scoop the yogurt into bowls or sundae glasses. Garnish with grilled pineapple, sprinkle some coconut and mint sprigs and serve immediately.

5.20 Grilled angel food cake with strawberries in balsamic

Prep time: 15 min

Serves: 4

Ingredients:

- 1 1/2 lb. of strawberries

- 1 tbsp. of sugar

- 2 tbsp. of balsamic vinegar

- 1 cup of whipped cream (optional)

- 1 store-bought angel food cake

Directions:

- Toss strawberries with sugar and balsamic vinegar in a medium bowl. Allow it to stand at room temperature for at least thirty min, occasionally stirring, until sugar dissolves.

- Meanwhile, preheat an outdoor grill to medium for direct grilling. Cut Angel food cake into six wedges.

- Place cake on the hot grill rack and cook for 3 to 4 minutes, rotating once or until lightly toasted on both sides. Spoon the strawberries with their juice into six dessert dishes. Arrange grilled cake on plates alongside strawberries; if desired, top with whipped cream.

5.21 Chocolate, banana and hazelnut pizza

Prep time: 26 min

Serves: 8

Ingredients:

- 1 lb. of fresh pizza dough

- 2 bananas

- 1/2 cup of chocolate and hazelnut spread like Nutella

Directions:

- Preheat outdoor grill to medium-low for covered, direct grilling.

- Divide dough into four equal halves. Spread and flatten 1 slice of dough to around 1/8-inch thickness with fingertips on one end of an oiled cookie sheet. (The edge does not have to be straight.)

- Rep with other pieces of dough on the same sheet. Repeat with the leftover dough and a second oiled baking sheet.

- Arrange the four dough bits, oiled side down, on a grill grate. Cook for 2 or 3 minutes, or before grill marks emerge on the underside (dough must be stiffened and puff).

- Turn crusts over with the tongs, remove from grill, and place on the work surface, grilled side up. Divide the chocolate hazelnut spread equally across crusts, leaving a ½ inch border, and place back on grill grate.

- Cover the grill and continue cooking pizzas for a further 3-4 minutes, or until the undersides are uniformly browned and baked through.

- Transfer to a cutting board; cover pizzas with banana slices and serve

5.22 Grilled Peach Melba

Prep time: 15 min

Serves: 4

Ingredients:

- large ripe peaches
- 1 tbsp. of sugar
- 1/2 pt. of raspberries
- 1 1/2 cups of vanilla ice cream

Directions:

- Preheat outdoor grill to medium-high for direct grilling.

- Place peach halves on the hot grill grate and cook for 5 to 6 minutes, rotating once, or until gently charred and soft.

- In the meantime, prepare the sauce: Mash half of the raspberries with a fork in a cup. Remaining raspberries should be stirred in.

- Place a peach half in each of four dessert bowls and top with ice cream scoop and raspberry sauce and serve.

5.23 Grilled pound cake with Meyer lemon simple syrup

Prep time: 1 hour and 20 min

Serves: 8

Ingredients:

- 1 cup of granulated sugar

- 1/2 cup of fresh juice from 4 lemons
- 1 tablespoon of Meyer lemon zest
- 2 cups of frozen thawed whipped topping
- 1 (12oz.) of loaf pound cake
- ¼ cup (2 oz.) of softened salted butter
- 2 tbsp. of cooking spray
- ½ cups of water

Directions:

- In a saucepan over medium-high heat, bring water and sugar to a boil. Cook, often stirring, till sugar dissolves entirely, around 3 minutes.
- Take the pan off the heat. Stir in juice and lemon zest, cover and chill for 1 hour.
- Cut cake into 8 slices (1 1/4-inch thick). Butter the cake slices.
- Preheat grill to a medium-high temperature (400°F–450°F). Arrange cake slices on a grill rack that has been sprayed with cooking spray.
- Grill, uncovered, for approximately 3 minutes on each side. Serve slices on small plates and drizzle lemon syrup, and whipped topping dollop.

5.24 Grilled chocolate and raspberry dessert sandwiches

Prep time: 10 min

Serves: 4

Ingredients:

- 8 (1/4-inch) slices of Italian, Portuguese or round sourdough bread
- ¼ cup of seedless raspberry preserves
- 12 (0.53 oz.) packages of truffle-filled dark chocolate squares or 2 (1.55 oz.) of milk chocolate bars
- 2 tbsp. of Course sea salt (optional)
- 8 teaspoons of butter

Directions:

- Preheat grill to a moderate temperature (300°). In one side of the bread strips, spread the raspberry preserves. In the center of four slices, place two chocolate squares or half of a milk chocolate cookie. Place leftover bread slices on top. On the outside of each slice, spread approximately 2 teaspoons butter.

- Grill sandwiches for 2 minutes on one side; gently switch and grill for another 2 minutes on the other side, or until bread is toasted, and the chocolate is warm. Allow sandwiches to stand for 1 to 2 minutes before slicing in half and serve

Conclusion

Food science is difficult, even though following the simplest recipe. There is absolutely no doubt that meat cooked over an open flame tastes incredible, and there is also no doubt that grilled poultry, fish and meat, provide fewer calories and fat than their fried counterparts while maintaining their juiciness and flavor. As a result, it is the healthiest method of making your favorite food. For example, grilled burgers produce approximately 1 gram less fat and ten fewer calories than burgers fried in a deep fryer and drippings. Grilling is highly recommended for every home chef looking to advance their passion. The grill's aroma, the flame's hiss is mind-blowing. Grilling in the backyard is a lot of fun. It is one of the summer's biggest pleasures. It makes no difference what you place on there. It has an incredible aroma and flavor. After all, one of the rules of healthier restaurant dining is to order "grilled" meals rather than "cooked." This is since grilled food is usually a better option due to the absence of dripping grease or batter coating. Besides, there is something about grilling that enhances the appearance and flavor of beef. Is it the smoky smell, the variety of marinades, the grill marks that shape the beef, and the flavorful taste that results from cooking something quickly over the high heat? You can try hundreds of recipes, with not only meat but also with vegetables and other foods.

This book contains a set of recipes that we believe work well together and are perfect for grilling. When you have more time, the tips, on the other hand, demonstrate how to grill properly and prepare plates and even main courses for larger parties or special occasions. Therefore, if you want to make your food even more delicious and enjoy delectable recipes, you should not hesitate to purchase your very own Grill.

9 781513 685700